UNVEILING SHADOWS OF COERCIVE CONTROL

KIMBERLY MOSBY

Copyright © 2024 by Kimberly Mosby

Published by Kimberly Mosby in Partnership with

Bold Publishing

(https://www.boldpublishings.com)

Book Design by Opeyemi Ikuborije

Edited by Donna and Tony Stark Policci

Publisher's Note:

Without limiting the rights under copyright reserved above, no part of this publication may be reproduced, stored in or introduced into a retrieval system, or transmitted, in any form, or by any means (electronic, mechanical, photocopying, recording, or otherwise), without the prior written permission of both the copyright owner and the publisher of the book.

Manufactured in the United States of America

ISBN: 979-8-9917255-3-8

Library of Congress Control Number: 2024910437

Follow Kimberly Mosby

Social Media Outlets:

Facebook: @unveilingshadows
Instagram: @unveiledshadows
TikTok: @unveiltheshadows
YouTube: @unveilingshadowspodcast
X: @shadowsunveiled
Substack: @unveilingshadows

CONTENTS

Dedication I

Acknowledgment Iii

Foreword - Reed And Sherrie Crowe V

Preface Vii

About The Author Xi

Introduction 1

Chapter One: A Symphony Of Intrusion 3

Chapter Two: Web Of Secrets: Dismantling Piece By Piece 9

Chapter Three: Unraveling Roots 19

Chapter Four: Echoes Of Independence 25

Chapter Five: Unraveling Threads 29

Chapter Six: Determined. 39

Chapter Seven: The Illusion Of Normalcy 43

Chapter Eight: Unseen Forces 53

Chapter Nine: Shadows Of Deceit 57

Chapter Ten: Web Of Allegiances 61

Chapter Eleven: The Dance Of Shadows. 65

Chapter Twelve: Resilience And Farewell 75

Chapter Thirteen: Beneath The Surface 79

Chapter Fourteen: Finding Sanctuary And Purpose 93

Valuable Support And Guidance For Readers 99

DEDICATION

This book is dedicated to my daughter Lydia, whose radiant spirit and unwavering inspiration continue to guide me, even from the afterlife. Though separated by the boundaries of life and death, your impact on my soul transcends the physical, shaping the very essence of this literary journey. In every word penned, in every tale spun, your lasting influence echoes, a testament to our timeless bond. Though you no longer walk this life with us, your presence remains a source of strength and inspiration, illuminating the path of creativity and love. This work is a tribute to you, Lydia, my eternal muse -Queen of the Street.

ACKNOWLEDGMENT

Completing this undertaking would not have been possible without the unwavering support of my Uncle Reed and Aunt Sherrie. Their suggestion to start this writing journey and their steadfast presence during the most challenging times of my life have been invaluable.

A special acknowledgment goes to Mel, Lizz, Jackie, Sam, TenAce, and Natalie for nourishing my soul during the Wolf Moon retreat and encouraging me to complete this manuscript.

I sincerely thank Chris for his steadfast support, friendship, and valuable insights, which enriched the pages of this book.

Last but not least, I want to acknowledge my dear friend Heather, who not only opens my eyes but also elevates my spirits with her unwavering friendship and encouragement.

And, of course, Emily, where would I be without your support? Thank you.

FOREWORD - REED AND SHERRIE CROWE

Kim's remarkable journey is not just a tale of determination; it's a testament to the unyielding spirit that resides within her. Kim defied the odds from the beginning with a steadfast resolve that sets her apart.

One of Kim's defining characteristics is her committed response to skepticism. If ever told she couldn't achieve something, her reaction was never defeat but determination. She embraces challenges with such enthusiasm and reverence that they can leave one in awe.

Through the years, Kim has faced numerous trials, each met with an unparalleled determination to succeed. Balancing the responsibilities of single motherhood with pursuing her education, she earned her business degree while raising three children and working full-time; Kim's journey doesn't stop there.

In the face of financial crises and the constant background noise of cautionary voices urging restraint, Kim embarked on the journey of entrepreneurship, founding multiple successful businesses. Her ventures defied the odds and thrived in adversity, a testament to her resilience and foresight.

Even today, as she navigates the complexities of business in an ever-changing landscape, Kim remains undeterred. She meets challenges with innovation, setbacks with resilience, and obstacles with unshakable determination.

Kim's story is not just about triumph over adversity; it's evidence of the power of perseverance, the strength of character, and the unwavering belief in oneself. In her story, we find inspiration, motivation, and a reminder that with dedication and courage, anything is achievable.

As you journey through Kim's story, may you find within it the same spirit that propels her forward – a spirit of resilience, determination, and unyielding belief in the power of possibility.

PREFACE

At some point in our lives, we've all faced betrayal or encountered attempts by others to impose their will upon us in undesirable ways. What sets Kim's story apart is the depth, scope, and sheer ruthlessness of those who sought to deprive her of her freedom, declare her incompetent, and strip her of her assets.

Within this narrative, you'll encounter emerging terms like *gang stalking*, *directed energy attacks/weapons*, *neuro-warfare*, *neurotechnology*, and more. While many are familiar with the frowned-upon MK-Ultra experiments of the past, Kim's story unveils a more contemporary version of clandestine attacks akin to MK-Ultra, aimed at evoking specific behaviors and discrediting her in general.

While such occurrences are not entirely new, what is new is the integration of cutting-edge technology with psychological, neurological, and chemical warfare tactics. Even more disturbing is the potential for these methods to be turned against ordinary citizens to exert control over them.

Initially, as I heard Kim's story and gave thought to its implications, I wanted to ascertain its plausibility. To my dismay, I discovered that, indeed, it is possible. For instance, one account involves a perplexing "light show," which could be produced through the dispersion of vaporous clouds or powders combined with projection/image sources upon closer examination. Even scientists' development of holographic images [1] underscores the plausibility of such events, whose means and methods are often shrouded in secrecy.

Furthermore, you'll encounter references to substances like Lucifer Yellow, which are used to trace cell absorption pathways. This, coupled with electromagnetic waves from directed energy weapons, constitutes an emerging domain known as neuro-warfare, distinct from psychological warfare yet employed against Kim.

The utilization of these methods alongside coercive psychological tactics, as seen in the community therapeutic approach to addiction weaponized against Kim, transcends mere privacy violations and breaches of basic human decency. It aims to isolate individuals, forcing them into corners where escape seems futile.

Kim's journey may venture into territories some find unsettling. Nevertheless, she does not have an addiction; she grapples with the aftermath of familial betrayal trauma and court-imposed hardships. Despite facing hypervigilance, anxiety, obsession, and depression, she courageously confronts her accusers and endeavors to reclaim her agency.

As you embark on this tumultuous journey with Kim, I implore you to maintain an open mind. Understand that her parents wield significant wealth and political power, capable of exerting immense pressure and influence, often inadvertently harming their own kin. This underscores the potential repercussions for Kim should she become an outspoken critic of specific topics.

---

1. Speculation about programs like Project Blue Beam suggests the capability to create hyper-realistic holograms combined with infrasonic weapons to manipulate human perception. According to some experts, these holograms could even possess temporary solidity and be used to project religious or alien figures as part of psychological operations. Read the article and watch the video of former FBI Agent John Desouza here: http://tiny.cc/bluebeam

The combination of familial dynamics, external pressures, coercion, and loss forms the backdrop against which Kim's story unfolds – a tale of resilience, introspection, grappling with forces beyond her control, and the desires imposed by others that she cannot stop.

Chris Peterson

ABOUT THE AUTHOR

Kimberly Mosby is a seasoned leader with a track record of success in management across diverse industries. Born in Helena, Montana, Kimberly's journey epitomizes resilience and adaptability.

She graduated a year early from East High School. A cum laude graduate of the University of Phoenix with degrees in Business Management and Business Administration. Kimberly excelled in roles such as Owner, Title Officer, and Escrow Officer at Gateway Title, where she spearheaded innovative initiatives like paperless closing systems.

Prior to Gateway Title, Kimberly held positions at prominent organizations like Cox Communications, Countrywide Home Loans, and First American, consistently exceeding goals and building strong client relationships.

Kimberly continues to significantly impact her community and beyond through her multifaceted career and dedication to excellence. She is the proud author of her debut book, *Unveiling Shadows of Coercive Control*

INTRODUCTION

In this book, I'm sharing my intense personal experience with coercive control - a severe type of mental manipulation. **I wrote much of this book in a form that reads like diary entries. It will make more sense and cause less confusion if you keep that in mind as you read. I have changed names of certain individuals and organizations to respect their privacy.**

The events and timelines reveal a backdrop of unsettling attempts to institutionalize me in a psychiatric facility when I didn't need to be there. This was all part of a calculated plan to induce mental illness and distort my reality by isolating me from my support network and cutting me off from my friends and family. All done to satisfy a need for power and dominance over my business.

This book shows how deeply coercive control can affect a person's mind. It reveals ways some people try to control others, both mentally and physically. Going through this was incredibly traumatic for me. I had to constantly fight against people, trying to change how I saw the world and control every part of my life.

As you read, you'll see the dark side of manipulation and the complex tricks used to break someone's spirit. This isn't just my story -I want you to understand what victims of coercive control go through. I want you to recognize the signs, to know that this dark underbelly

2 | Introduction

of manipulation exists in our world. Maybe you'll see it happening to someone you know or realize it's happening to you.

I hope this book helps spread awareness about coercive control and encourages people to care about this issue. Come with me as I take you through my difficult journey. You'll see how I fought against those who tried to break me down and how I overcame it, not just surviving but stronger and more resilient. Let's dive in, shall we?

One last thing before we start. If you scan this QR Code it will take you to a "resources" page on my website. Please watch the two videos at the top for proof that what you are about to read is credible. The direct URL is: https://unveilingshadows.com/resources/.

CHAPTER ONE

A SYMPHONY OF INTRUSION

As I look back on the chaotic chapters of my life, one theme keeps repeating: a relentless invasion of my personal space. This unwelcome intrusion, orchestrated by unseen forces, went far beyond anything ethical or justifiable. It threw me into a nightmare where privacy was a distant memory, and my sense of control was slipping away.

The Unwelcomed Beginning

It all started when I noticed some holes in the walls of my porch and thought I had a termite problem. I mentioned it to my neighbor Peter Pottinger, wondering if he had similar issues. He made a snide remark, instead of giving me a straight answer. I called Terminix and they told me I had wood burrowing beetles and carpenter ants. They treated it and I thought the problem was over. Not long after Terminex left, I began feeling weak and could hardly get up off of my couch. No matter how I tried, I could not shake the heavy feeling, which lasted about 24 hours. That was only the beginning.

What followed next was a disturbing feeling of uncertainty about everything. The boundaries that once safeguard the sanctity of my personal life, now felt shattered as I experienced several insults of invasion.

Looking back, the invasion went beyond mere violation of privacy; it marked a deliberate and premeditated attack on the very essence of who I am. The safe-haven of my personal space transformed into a battleground, where an undercover war was waged against my autonomy and well-being. No one around me seemed to notice what was taking place; that led me to question everything and everyone's behavior.

Every aspect of my existence seemed subject to interference – from personal relationships to professional pursuits, nothing was immune. As I assessed each person I encountered, I saw some, not as passive actors but as active manipulators skillfully exerting their influence over me.

They carefully crafted a narrative that aimed to rationalize their shameful actions, manipulating circumstances to justify the unjustifiable and hide their true agenda.

Stripping of Assets

The invasion into my life played out like an ominous melody; each note a reminder of the attempts to strip away my life's work trying to destroy the balance between my financial security and personal safety. I found myself fixing things repeatedly, only to find that it wasn't enough, or having to purchase things that usually last me years.

My financial assets, that used to be symbols of my security and hard work, were now being targeted to dismantle the foundation of my entire life. This violation crept up on me: at first I thought I was just having bad luck and things were falling apart. Not knowing I was being pressured to spend money on expensive repairs, services, and seemingly urgent purchases that only drained me further. Every new expense left me feeling frustrated.

Remarkably, this went beyond the loss of my money, it attacked the very essence of who I am. I had once prided myself on being a breadwinner,but now I was feeling insecure and helpless in the face of an enemy I could not see.

Losing the money felt like a direct hit to my independence, shaking the very foundation of who I was. The loss of money was just the surface of a more heinous attack on my sense of control and self-worth. What was once a private part of my life became a public affair, spilling over into my emotions and messing with my head.

A Stark Reminder of Financial Invasion

I learned that financial stability and personal security are intertwined – an attack on one can have effects in every part of your life. The threads that hold our lives together are fragile, and when pulled, they can unravel, leaving behind a mess of uncertainty and chaos.

Tampering with Deliveries

As the intrusion into my life grew more intense, it extended to my deliveries – Amazon packages and other shipments appeared tampered with. What used to be the simple joy of receiving a package turned into a source of fear and vulnerability. Each parcel arrived looking torn, disturbed, even partially opened as though someone had gone through it before delivering it to me.

Lucifer Yellow and Other Chemicals

I remember feeling like the very air I was breathing was contaminated, taking a toll on my physical and mental health. Later, I found out that Lucifer Yellow was being used to control and manipulate me. Lucifer Yellow is a vivid fluorescent dye, often used in scientific studies to see how cells respond to treatments like electroporation. Electroporation is a scientific technique often used in scientific studies to test how cells respond to certain treatments like electroporation[2] and magnetoporation[3]. Normally, the membrane acts like a protective skin around the cell, controlling what goes in and out. Lucifer Yellow can temporarily make the membrane a bit "leaky" so things like dyes, medicines, or DNA can get inside. It's particularly valuable in neuroscience, and pharmacology, where researchers use it to track and study intricate processes within living cells.

The dye has been mentioned in discussions about mind control and psychological manipulation, particularly in the context of theories surrounding government experiments (e.g., MK-Ultra).

---

2. Where the cells are briefly exposed to a small, controlled electric shock that makes tiny holes in the cell membrane, so things (like DNA or medicine) can get inside. After the process, the cell membrane usually repairs itself quickly, closing - those tiny holes.

3. This technique uses magnetic nanoparticles—tiny particles with magnetic properties. When these nanoparticles are mixed with the substance scientists want to insert into the cell (like a drug), the particles act like tiny delivery vehicles. A magnetic field is applied to pull the particles towards the cells, and the magnetic force helps open the cell membrane to let the drug inside.

Direct Electromagnetic Warfare (DEW)

The height of this attack came with direct electromagnetic warfare[4] (DEW), a technological attack aimed at my very existence. These invisible waves of interference turned my peaceful life upside down, causing physical and emotional distress. It was an assault on who I am, an attempt to erase my identity through a stream of unseen forces.

As this story unfolds, I invite you to walk with me through the corridors of these attacks, where each wave of assaults leaves a haunting mark on my life and almost extinguishes the essence of who I am.

---

4. Recent reports from the Department of Defense confirm the existence of Directed Energy Weapons, including those deployed in space to target adversaries. Such technologies can be used to manipulate or disable equipment and potentially affect biological systems. Dept. of Defense Secretary Mark Esper CONFIRMED Directed Energy Weapons usage by the Air Force at the Air Force Association's Virtual Air, Space & Cyber Conference on Sept 16, 2020.

CHAPTER TWO

WEB OF SECRETS: DISMANTLING PIECE BY PIECE

A Troubled Relationship and New Encounters

My relationship with Garth Meyers, who worked for Shotspotter[5], came to an end in February 2019 after 22 months filled with distrust and tears. Something always felt off in that relationship, leaving me with a lingering sense of unease. It didn't help that the American Civil Liberties Union had issues with Garth and Shotspotter for violating privacy rights. Perhaps my sense of unease about Garth was an omen? Two months before our relationship ended, he gave me a 24 karat gold bracelet for Christmas. We were in one of my family members' homes and when I opened the box, the look of distaste on one of my relatives' faces struck me to the core. At the time I thought it might have been jealousy. As time went on - and the involvement of people closest to me in dismantling my life became apparent - I believe the look may actually have been because gold can help repel magnetic fields.

In November 2020, my therapist urged me to start dating. He said I was in a good spot and ready. He also told me that now (during the

---
5. Shotspotter is now known as https://www.soundthinking.com

"plandemic") would be the perfect time to start because the necessity to talk over the phone or facetime to get to know each other would be safer. So, following that advice, I met Samuel Owen by chance on Match.com.

Samuel was a recent graduate of The Other Side Academy (TOSA), which is a program presented as a transformative rehabilitation program designed to assist individuals grappling with addiction, homelessness, and criminal behavior. This long-term residential program spans 30 months, providing a structured environment where participants can learn essential life skills and vocational training. TOSA targets those who have often cycled through the criminal justice system, with many students having faced numerous arrests – averaging around 25. The program emphasizes accountability and personal growth through a peer-driven model that fosters community support and mentorship.

At TOSA, participants engage in rigorous training that includes both personal management and relationship skills, such as accountability, dependability, and self-governance. They work full-time in various vocational training schools and businesses run by the Academy, which helps sustain the program financially while providing practical work experience. Activities range from operating a thrift store to managing a moving company, ensuring that every participant contributes to the community.

The Academy's approach is rooted in the principles of a classic therapeutic community, where peer influence takes precedence over traditional therapeutic methods. This model encourages participants to confront their past behaviors and learn from one another in a "supportive environment.' TOSA requires a deep commitment for individuals seeking to break free from cycles of addiction and crime, equipping them with the tools necessary for a healthier, more productive life.

But TOSA is very similar to Synanon. Synanon was a controversial organization founded in 1958 by Charles E. "Chuck" Dederich Sr. in Santa Monica, California. Initially established as a drug rehabilitation program, it evolved over time into a new religious movement and eventually became known as one of the most dangerous cults in American history.

Samuel brought drugs into the mix, claiming it was a way to blur the lines between friendship and what he called psychological warfare. He was a man caught up in a complicated web of secrets and unexpected consequences and was intrigued by the mysterious nature of TOSA. He was drawn into its complex world, unaware of the secrets and challenges ahead. Little did he know that his life was deeply connected to the fate of this unusual institution.

As Samuel became more involved with TOSA, he felt like he was undergoing a relentless form of psychological warfare, a tough boot camp for the soul. Every day brought new struggles, forcing him to face his deepest fears. Yet, despite the chaos, there was a sense of purpose, a small hope that kept him going.

Samuel's Destined Path and the Unfolding Intrigue

Strangely, it seemed like Samuel's journey to The Other Side Academy was meant to be, as if fate had decided his path long before he arrived. He discovered that his father had met the mysterious founder of TOSA just days before Samuel was forced into the program. This encounter added more mystery to Samuel's story, raising more questions than it answered.

Despite the uncertainty, he pushed forward, determined to uncover the secrets surrounding him. Each day, he dug deeper into his own mind, facing the demons within and building a strong resolve to create his own path, no matter the cost.

As he navigated the challenges at TOSA, he realized that his journey wasn't just about surviving but about transformation. The obstacles he faced and the secrets he uncovered about the facility all shaped his reality. In the midst of the chaos and uncertainty, I suppose he found a glimmer of hope, a guiding light leading him toward a new beginning.

But Samuel Owen's hidden agenda added a new layer of complexity to the story. It became clear that he targeted me because of our discussions about my resistance to addiction. What started as a friendship eventually took a dark turn and he introduced me to methamphetamines.[6]

My experimentation with methamphetamines, which affected me differently than most people due to my mild ADHD, became a key part of the unfolding intrigue. On the few occasions when Samuel introduced the drug into our interactions, I never missed a night of sleep. I was still getting six to eight hours a night, the only thing that methamphetamine did was to focus me. It has the opposite effect on most people, where they stay up for days.

The Spark of a Tweet and HOA Manipulations

In early 2021, a single tweet I posted ignited a chain of unexpected events. On Twitter, I expressed my frustration with what I saw as the overreach of a powerful figure named Loki, the World Health Organization (WHO), and the World Economic Forum (WEF) in

---

[6]. The inclusion of methamphetamine experimentation is important, as it is a recurring theme among the Targeted that few have the courage to disclose. It is apparent to me that street drugs are used as carriers for BCI technology. Once the Target has engaged in this activity, they are pre-qualified for reputational harm, and the BCI experiments/torture can begin. - John Phillips author of The Electromagnetic Revolution & Federal Targeted Individual Program. Also interviewed by Kevin Daniells for the documentary on targeted individuals

controlling my health rights. Little did I know that simple post would lead me down a path filled with mystery and intrigue.

On March 4, 2021, the local Forest Dale condominium homeowners association (HOA) changed the rules, stating that homeowners couldn't put locks on their utility closets, where my furnace and water purification system were located. This marked the beginning of what I believe was a targeted effort against me. The HOA started changing the bylaws to suit their agenda, and apparently this enabled them to contaminate my water supply with something yellow. I pulled out my filter a few months later and it was completely yellow. This meant I had been forced to bathe in it, drink it, and live in a saturated environment.

A New Encounter and Suspicious Activities

September 2022 was a turning point when I met Trevor Burrows, an unexpected figure in this unfolding drama. Burrows, an FBI agent, came into my life because of a last-minute seat change on my return flight from my cousin's wedding in Montana. Our relationship became more than just professional – we also became *friends with benefits*.

During our time together, Burrows moved to Salt Lake City and asked for recommendations on local healthcare professionals. I suggested Dr. Sonny Renae, an alternative healthcare provider. Little did I know this innocent recommendation would connect different elements of the ongoing mystery.

Around the same time, I noticed a peculiar man I nicknamed ZZ Top because of his distinctive white beard. He was seen disposing of items in the dumpster and tampering with the public water system at the Wood Hollow complex near my condo. He was believed to work for the city and lived nearby in a house with unsettling decorations. The eerie similarity between ZZ Top and my neighbor at Forest Dale, Patrick Winter, made me suspicious of their connection.

My sharp observational skills and strong memory helped me notice patterns and connections around me. ZZ Top's familiar face reminded me of Patrick Winter, who was linked to a community therapeutic approach but was suspected of working against my interests with another individual, Peter Pottinger. Peter and his wife purchased the condo upstairs from mine in 2019 and did some remodeling prior to moving in. I'll talk more about him in chapter five.

A Strange Weekend and Unsettling Alerts

On April 14, 2023, my hairstylist, Vigil, stayed with me while she was in town. That evening, we used MDMA and mushrooms and set intentions for our experience. During her stay, Vigil mentioned she was allergic to shrimp and metallic eyeshadow and suggested I mix my lotions. She also had clothing delivered from Shein to my condo, possibly to show some sort of residency, even though her salon was just up the street.

However, during our weekend, a strange alert disrupted our conversations. On April 24, 2023, my Nest Protect system sent a warning about an absence of check-ins at my home, adding an unexpected layer of mystery to the weekend.

The next day, April 25, 2023, another odd event occurred. After fixing my garbage disposal, I found myself dealing with a clogged drain and had to call Friendly Home Service for help. At the same time, the HOA decided to reduce the water pressure, claiming it was necessary.

This decision triggered a series of plumbing issues that worsened my already complicated situation. The water problems lingered into

May, with yellowish-orange rings appearing in my toilet bowls just two weeks after cleaning them, suggesting that my water had been contaminated with something – likely Lucifer Yellow – since this had never happened before.

An Unusual Weekend and New Mysteries

The weekend of April 28, 2023, took an unexpected turn for Myles Gardner and me. He was the president of the chamber where I served as an ambassador for 6 months. He had a crush on me but … he also had a friend who owned a company I'll call "Yearly Labs." That friend had a connection to Sonny Renae who forced me to take a drug test and found things in my blood that I am absolutely sure I never took.

What started as casual conversations and shared experiences quickly became something more unusual. We decided to try a unique "hippie-tripping" session, where I found myself sharing stories about the strange light shows and ghostly illuminations that had appeared in my condo at night. I took videos of these and even submitted them to an investigator as evidence.

I told Myles about these odd occurrences in the spirit of openness, creating a sense of intrigue and wonder. Myles listened closely as I described the eerie displays that had unfolded in my home.

As May rolled in, from the 8th to the 12th, a new chapter of uncertainty began. I called Priority Labs to conduct a mold test after noticing strange substances coming from the air jets that looked like mold. To my relief, the results showed that the mysterious substance was more like paper than mold. The air in my home at Forest Dale actually had less mold than the outside air, leaving me puzzled.

During this time, the combination of ghostly stories, home alerts, and unexpected plumbing problems added to the mystery of my daily life, creating a narrative of intrigue within Forest Dale's walls.

On May 18, 2023, something strange happened outside my porch. My Wyze camera captured a peculiar dance of leaves, moving in ways that didn't make sense with the wind. This made me suspicious, making it seem like even nature was conspiring with the strange events at Forest Dale.

As if guided by an unseen force, the unsettling feeling of being watched grew stronger when I noticed someone hiding behind a large pine tree I ominously dubbed "Big Daddy." To me, the tree symbolized something – it felt like a protector. (Once I tossed a magnet at it, and it stuck!)[7] Peering at this figure, I didn't know who it was at first. Then I realized it was Samuel Owen. When I called out to him, he quickly crouched down and scrambled out of sight, leaving me with more questions than answers.

The mysteries didn't end there. On May 19, 2023, I had a therapy appointment with Jared, a therapist my parents had recommended. During our session, I told him about a strange encounter with my orthodontist, Dr. Errol, who had unexpectedly suggested I get double crowns on two adjacent teeth, even though I wasn't in pain or in need of the procedure.

Jared's response added to my skepticism. With a touch of sarcasm, he suggested I get a second opinion from a nearby dentist, reinforcing my disbelief in the odd dental advice. Interestingly, Jared revealed that he was a supporter of The Other Side Academy (TOSA) and admired the program's success stories.

---

7. I later experimented by tossing about 100 different magnets at this tree, with about 99% of them sticking. I ended up using some other large magnets to throw off the magnetic field by throwing them on top of the metal carport located to the north of my condominium.

As the mysteries within and beyond Forest Dale continued to pile up, the connection between seemingly unrelated events heightened the sense of intrigue. The dancing leaves, the mysterious figure, and the strange dental encounter painted a surreal picture of my life. Little did I know that these events were just the beginning of a deeper deception.

As the story of Forest Dale unfolded, an unsettling revelation about gang stalking emerged, shedding light on a hidden world of terror. Gang-stalking, rooted in notorious practices like the FBI's COINTELPRO and the Gestapo's methods, has evolved into a global network embedded within the surveillance apparatus of various intelligence agencies. COINTELPRO[8], short for Counterintelligence Program, was a series of covert and often illegal operations conducted by the Federal Bureau of Investigation (FBI) from 1956 to 1971.

The intrigue deepened when NSA whistle-blower Kenzy Linton revealed that Lockheed Martin, a defense contractor, allegedly oversees gang-stalking operations in 47 of the 50 U.S. states. This revelation highlighted the disturbing influence of private companies in orchestrating systematic harassment.

Since 2001, western intelligence agencies have seen a surge in recruitment, often targeting people from low-income backgrounds. These covert operations are further concealed by off-the-books payments, sometimes using untraceable methods like gift cards.

A troubling development in this secretive network is the rise of Pay-Stalking – an app-driven system that turns stalking into a profitable

---

8. COINTELPRO was initiated in 1956 with the primary goal of disrupting the activities of the Communist Party of the United States. However, its scope expanded over time to target various domestic political and activist groups that the FBI deemed subversive. The program was exposed in 1971 when activists burglarized an FBI office in Media, Pennsylvania, and released confidential files to the press. Despite its official end, there are allegations that COINTELPRO-type activities have continued under different names. The program's history serves as a cautionary tale about government overreach and the potential abuse of power in the name of national security.

activity. This encouragement of stalking raises serious ethical concerns about intelligence practices.

In the U.S., many potential gang-stalkers were likely drawn from those who fell into financial hardship during the 2008 financial crisis and became dependent on food stamps. The size of this group, comparable to the population of Spain, suggests a vast resource available for what is described as an "asset-stripping" operation against productive members of society.

The tactics used in gang stalking go beyond psychological harassment: break-ins, sabotage of vehicles, death threats, and mock assassination attempts push victims into a constant state of fear.

As Forest Dale's story continues to unfold, revelations about gang-stalking cast a dark shadow, exposing a network that operates beyond conventional understanding. I was left to confront the unsettling reality that there were hidden forces at work.

CHAPTER THREE

UNRAVELING ROOTS

The summer of 2023 brought new challenges to my living space, starting with a clash between my condominium and the holly bushes growing in front of it. When the bushes became overgrown, I emailed the Homeowners' Association (HOA) to request trimming. To my surprise, the HOA told me it was my responsibility. As I cut them down, I noticed the bright yellow roots growing rapidly, raising more questions than answers.

But the holly bushes weren't the only issue. The wrought iron in front of my side of the building had deteriorated, a sign of deeper problems lurking beneath the surface.

On June 30, 2023, I hosted a wine evening with friends and family. The idea came from Karen Lane, a former confidante, and was organized by Alfred Simon. At the time, I believed this was simply a casual gathering for family and friends. The true intention however was a cover for a community therapy intervention - and I realized this just a week or so before the event.

To keep control over the situation, I held the event outside, which upset some family members. They didn't know my reluctance to host inside was based on a deeper understanding of the potential dangers to me from such a gathering. I watched my mother and neighbors struggling to get inside my condominium, to wield their plan to drop Lucifer Yellow for contact tracing. Unbeknownst to them I had the locks changed. The tension between wanting a family celebration and avoiding unwanted intervention set the stage for an evening that blurred the lines between hospitality and coercion.

The use of Lucifer Yellow, a substance linked to psychological experiments[9], made me uneasy and I was suspicious of them and didn't want those tracing in my home.

As the holly bushes lay trimmed and the wrought iron quietly rusted, the echoes of that evening lingered, hinting at conflicts that extended beyond my home. Little did I know that these events were just part of a more complex narrative waiting to unravel.

A Veil of Concern

July 3, 2023, marked a turning point in the ongoing mystery at Forest Dale. My parents and children visited, but two individuals from the U of U Behavioral Health Facility also showed up, adding an unsettling element to the day. Later, I learned from my medical records that my family had contacted the Medical Crisis Outreach Team (MCOT).

The visit felt like an interrogation, with probing questions about my mental health. It revealed a harsh truth – I was overwhelmed trying to support my two children at Gateway Title, Lance's girlfriend, Abigail Rivers, and my confidante Karen Lane at Apex Title, which was

---

9. LY's role in tracing neuronal pathways can contribute to understanding the biological underpinnings of mental health disorders. Research involving neuronal morphology and synaptic connections may provide insights into conditions like schizophrenia or bipolar disorder, where altered neural connectivity is observed.

straining my finances. I had to dissolve Apex Title to simply stay afloat, which only increased the tension and my sense of an impending threat.

During the evaluation, I mentioned radiation spots on the floor, but my concerns were dismissed as delusions. This disconnect between my experiences and their interpretation left me feeling misunderstood and frustrated.

The visit took another turn when my stepfather tried to lighten the mood by commenting on my social media videos. However, his compliment was met with a disapproving glare from my mother, (now ex-mother), creating an uncomfortable atmosphere.

The evaluation, carefully documented as evidence, highlighted the profound challenges and misunderstandings I faced at Forest Dale. No matter how I tried to make sense of what was going on around me, more deception and suspicions came up. The line between reality and perception became increasingly blurred, leaving me to navigate a confusing and often unsettling reality.

Shadows of Doubt

As June ended and July began, the uncertainty at Forest Dale continued to grow. My business development manager, Mes Sine, and I had a candid conversation at the office. I confided in him about the unsettling contact tracing with Lucifer Yellow, hoping for some understanding. None was provided. Yet, the next day, a meeting with Dr. Sonny Renae brought more discomfort, as he urged me to keep certain matters, like Lucifer Yellow, to myself. His words, though practical, hinted at the potential dangers of speaking out. I soon realized that information had already reached Dr. Renae, and the confidentiality I expected seemed compromised.

Dr. Renae suggested that taking a vacation might help, but this only added to the complexity. He agreed to look into a radiation test when I asked for it. I asked because I had videos of me using a radiation detector in my residence and the levels reading off the charts. However, during a urinalysis, unexpected results showed substances I am sure I hadn't consumed, casting doubt on the integrity of the test.

In July, I noticed that food deliveries weren't packaged as they usually were, and I suspected drugs were being placed in my orders, which could explain the strange results of my test. Dr. Renae pressured me to come back for another test, but I decided to cancel.

The receptionist, Farrah, conveyed Dr. Renae's insistence that I take the test, which made me uneasy. Researching his background, I found out about his involvement in addiction recovery, raising ethical concerns. He pried into my business and was questioning me about my use with experimental drugs. He told me how he saved "some guy" and how he now made two-million dollars a year because of his successful intervention into this man's life. I got the idea that he was now after me. Wanting to use me as another test subject.

After doing some research I found him on a medical doctor review website as an addiction recovery specialist, which prompted me to give him a one-star review where I echoed my concerns about the breach of consent in these matters. And that he should probably let his victims know before he started meadling in their lives.

As the story of Forest Dale unfolded, the shadow of doubt deepened. The intersection of medical scrutiny, breaches of confidentiality, and unexpected revelations created an eerie atmosphere over what used to be familiar territory. The unraveling mystery now demanded a closer look at the people involved, leaving me to confront a reality that seemed increasingly hard to understand.

Echoes of Pursuit

July 5, 2023, was marked by a growing sense of being followed. This unease prompted me to visit a local locksmith to regain some control over my security. Changing the locks became a crucial step in the ongoing drama at Forest Dale.

When I arrived at the locksmith, I realized the urgency of my situation. The locks I wanted weren't immediately available, so we had to go to their warehouse. But I needed immediate action. Even though the desired locks weren't in stock, the technicians understood the urgency and quickly changed the patio door locks that day.

The sound of the new locks clicking into place brought a sense of empowerment, but the unease lingered. Strengthening the physical security of my home felt symbolic – an effort to control the tangible aspects of a situation spiraling into the intangible.

Yet, the feeling of being followed persisted, casting a shadow over the seemingly routine act of changing locks. Forest Dale, once a haven, now resonated with echoes of pursuit, urging me to stay vigilant. Each step in my home became a conscious assertion against the unseen forces.

CHAPTER FOUR

ECHOES OF INDEPENDENCE

As I walked through the familiar streets, the memories of that troubled weekend echoed in the quiet corners of the town. The horse racing track stood silent, and the off-track bar felt solemn, as if it, too, remembered the choices that had changed our lives.

Each step brought me closer to understanding the puzzle of Evanston on that Fourth of July as I sought to unravel the mysteries of that transformative weekend. This journey was not just a return to a place but a deeper exploration of the shadows that had lingered, waiting to be understood. The story unfolded – a tale of addiction, betrayal, and self-discovery – continuing my odyssey through coercive control.

In Evanston's strange atmosphere, the journey felt inevitable. The past echoed through every step, and soon, I found myself in a sex shop, driven by an uncontrollable urge. I recognized it as a planned act, a way to reclaim autonomy in the face of coerced experiences. The purchase of vibrators became a symbolic gesture of taking back control.

At the hotel, I was given a room on the top floor, which felt unsettling due to an unusual electromagnetic energy. The room's vibrations made me uneasy, so I requested a move to the other side of the hotel, away from electronic charging stations. However, the new room had the same eerie feel, as if coated in Lucifer Yellow. I decided to conduct an experiment with methamphetamine, fully aware that this would be one of the last chapters in a this saga.

The chemical rush coursed through me, and the room seemed to pulse with a peculiar energy, reflecting both my internal struggle and the external forces at play. The walls held secrets, and the shadows seemed to move in time with my heartbeat.

After leaving the hotel, I visited a smoke shop near the Wyoming Downs Off-Track Bar. There, I met Lily, the clerk, in what felt like a predestined encounter. The smoke shop, with its shelves full of paraphernalia, became the backdrop for our conversation – a moment where our stories converged.

Lily's piercing gaze suggested she understood more than she let on. Our lives seemed to intertwine as we talked, creating a shared narrative of experiences and resilience. The Off-Track Bar loomed in the background, a silent witness to the unfolding chapters of our respective journeys.

Amid these experiments and encounters, Evanston demanded exploration and introspection. The hotel's electromagnetic energy, the vibrators, and the meth experiment all became symbols of a tumultuous journey, inviting reflection on the interplay between external influences and personal choices. The narrative ventured deeper into the shadows, seeking understanding within the chaos.

During my conversation with Lily, I cautiously asked about Crystal Meth, seeking information rather than to purchase. I asked if she knew any local chemists familiar with the drug, emphasizing my curiosity about how it's made rather than wanting to buy it. She seemed to understand the complexities surrounding my quest for knowledge.

At one point, I asked Lily about a solvent for my car engine. To my surprise, she knew of one and offered it to me for free. As I stepped outside, the roar of old hotrods filled the air, amplified by the eerie presence of Lucifer Yellow. Lily mentioned a car show happening that weekend at the racetrack, further intertwining the story with the events unfolding in town.

I drove east of Evanston and pulled over to apply the acetone to my car engine. The strong scent filled the air, and as I resumed my journey, the magnetic interference that had plagued my car's screens seemed to ease – a subtle sign that the ritual had shifted the energies at play.

Later, I stopped at a local liquor store and bought a half gallon of cheap vodka – a symbolic gesture marking the end of this saga. As I drove past the Hampton Inn, memories of a traumatic weekend in 2022 resurfaced. Unable to resist the urge to cleanse, I pulled onto a side road and poured the vodka over my engine, hoping to purge the remnants of that turbulent chapter.

In the solitude of this ritual, a man in a red Jeep approached, curious about what I was doing. I explained that I was cleaning my engine, which seemed strange to him and perhaps others in the community. His gesture of indicating to others what I was doing reminded me of the isolation that often accompanies unconventional actions.

As the vodka evaporated into the Wyoming air, I felt a mix of liberation and vulnerability. The encounter with Lily, the cleansing ritual, and the curious onlookers marked a turning point in my journey through coercive control. The shadows still lingered, but I was determined to reclaim my agency amidst the echoes of a tumultuous past.

The Journey Back Home

The bizarre events in Evanston left a lasting impression on my journey through coercive control. Waking up to a group of teenagers surrounding my car felt surreal, prompting me to leave the town and return home, where the comforting presence of my cat awaited.

As I drove back to Salt Lake, the roar of semi-trucks on the road became a cacophony, and the rolling screens in my car resumed their familiar dance. The magnetic dust, a lingering reminder of Evanston's peculiar energies, amplified the noise, leading me to stop at Kimball Junction.

At a car wash, a blonde teenager with an intriguing grin directed me towards the automatic wash. Inside, the experience felt like a haunted house, mirroring the distortions of my journey.

Emerging from the wash, the screens continued their rebellious dance, refusing to be cleansed. The road home stretched ahead, winding through valleys of contemplation and unresolved emotions. The journey had become a quest for clarity amidst the echoes of Evanston.

Finally reaching home, the weight of the situation settled in, stirring a mix of emotions. The absurdity of recent events played out in my mind, a blend of humor and tragedy. Amidst the chaos, thoughts of my cat became a beacon of comfort, grounding me in familiarity.

As I unpacked the remnants of Evanston from my car, I couldn't help but reflect on the sheer absurdity of it all. The memories of that bizarre weekend would stay with me, a reminder of the resilience required to navigate the strange and unsettling forces at play. Despite the turmoil, the experience left me with a story marked by unexpected encounters, peculiar twists, and the unwavering spirit to face life's uncertainties with courage and a sense of humor.

CHAPTER FIVE

UNRAVELING THREADS

July 7, 2023, marked a crucial moment in my quest to understand and regain control over my life. Confronted with the unsettling presence of Lucifer Yellow, I began researching ways to counter its effects. After careful consideration, I ordered a 35% vinegar solution from Amazon, hoping it would help neutralize this mysterious substance. On the same day, I also made an appointment with an attorney named Lonny Raff, who had been recommended by my bookkeeper, Donna Harold.

When I met with Lonny, I explained what was happening. I told her it felt like my life had turned into some sort of game, with different teams betting on my every move, like a twisted simulation. I even shared my concerns that my children might be involved in real estate fraud. Lonny mentioned that real estate fraud was common and often involved altering last names to make them unrecognizable. She also told me about another woman who had been forced into a mental institution for 26 days against her will – a situation that was apparently happening to many successful, independent, single women.

I also did some background research on my neighbor, Peter Pottinger. It turned out he owned a company who I will call "Enriching Communities Through Technology" and a house just minutes away from Forest Dale, which struck me as odd. The background check also revealed that two people – Orpha York Hunter and Oscar M. Hunter – had shared his address despite both of them having passed away years earlier. Additionally, his first listed job title was "Major, Retired." When I shared this with my aunt and uncle, they looked up his LinkedIn profile, which I could no longer find, and told me that my condo was located in the center of a "Smart City" initiative and that Peter seemed fully invested in the idea.

However, on July 10, 2023, something unexpected happened. I received an email from Amazon saying I'd been refunded for the vinegar solution – an item I never returned. It became clear that my Amazon packages were being tampered with and experiencing unexplained delays. As I tried to piece together what was happening, I couldn't ignore the fact that the Amazon inland port just west of Salt Lake might be part of the problem, raising serious concerns about the integrity of the delivery process.

At the beginning of July, I also noticed something strange when logging into my work computer – other users, including one named Teresa, were on my system. No one by that name had ever worked with me or for the IT company I used. No one but me should have had administrative access to my computer. On July 18th, I sent a screenshot of active sessions to my personal email, which stated, "This account does not seem to be open in any other location," but it also showed that seven other authorized applications had been accessed on my work computer.

As this puzzle continued to unfold, July 20, 2023, brought another odd discovery. I noticed an unusual number of sprinkler heads placed right in front of my unit, so I emailed the Homeowners' Association (HOA) to find out why. The selective placement of these sprinklers made it clear that my living space was being singled out, deepening my curiosity about the motives behind these actions.

As these events began to connect, a complex picture emerged, blurring the lines between coincidence and intention. Each new piece of information drew me closer to the heart of a mystery that seemed to stretch far beyond my immediate surroundings. My determination to uncover the truth grew stronger as I worked to unravel the threads tying these seemingly unrelated occurrences together.

Shadows Deepen

August 1, 2023, became a turning point when I realized the full extent of my danger. That day it hit me I was a target and there was a bounty on my head. The person behind this terrifying situation was none other than Peter Pottinger, a figure who had quietly inserted himself into my life with dark intentions.

As this realization sank in, the world around me seemed to change. What was once familiar now felt like a maze of uncertainty, filled with hidden threats and motivations lurking in the shadows.

On August 4, 2023, what should have been a routine visit from a handyman revealed a sinister truth hidden within the walls of my condo. The day began with an unsettling feeling, a subtle unease that grew as I noticed strange boxes in the ceiling that hadn't been there before. These weren't ordinary boxes, and their sudden appearance was no accident. They seemed deliberately placed, casting doubt over my once-safe home.

Concerned, I called in Spunk's Handyman Service professionals to inspect these strange additions. Little did I know this decision would lead to uncovering a web of deception that had quietly woven itself into my life.

As the handyman carefully examined the boxes in my ceiling, his discovery was deeply unsettling. A vent, barely noticeable to the untrained eye, ran from inside my unit to the outside world. What struck me as odd was that no other unit in the condominium had such a vent. It was a lone channel connecting my living space to something unknown, leaving me feeling exposed and vulnerable.

The truth was more treacherous than I could have ever imagined. I soon realized that Peter Pottinger, a name that had meant little to me before, was the mastermind behind this covert operation. Lucifer Yellow was being pumped through my ventilation system, seeping into the air I breathed. The implications of this discovery were chilling, revealing a dark and malicious intent behind these actions.

A horrifying revelation followed – Samuel, an unwitting accomplice, had sprayed a yellow-orange substance on the walls after his showers. This was the residue of Lucifer Yellow, staining the walls of my master bath and turning the room into a chamber of deceit and danger. Samuel had also asked me if I'd visited Tracy Aviary at Liberty Park recently, suggesting I should go because it was one of my ex-stepfather's projects with the Pathright Organization. When I visited, I found the place in terrible condition, eerily empty. Around the same time, I noticed the community pool was closed in the middle of summer, along with many other pools in the area -likely because chlorine dissolves Lucifer Yellow.

The shadows that danced on the walls were not just figments of my imagination; they were the ominous signs of a truth I had been blind to. Samuel, once someone I trusted, now cast a terrifying light on the memories we shared in that space. The realization that my home had been invaded and my life manipulated was a bitter pill to swallow.

As I struggled to process this shocking truth, I knew I had to uncover the reasons behind this vile plot. Exposing the shadows would be painful, but it was something I could no longer avoid. The truth, once hidden, demanded to be brought to light, and I found myself on the brink of a journey into deep deception and danger.

August 5, 2023: Unveiling the Truth

August 5, 2023, brought another layer of complexity to this dark situation. I became aware of the insidious tactics being used under the guise of "community therapy." In my office, I found evidence of Lucifer Yellow.

When I questioned my youngest son, Leo, he unknowingly tried to erase the substance from my cabinets with a damp sponge. The water-streaked cabinets left a chilling reminder of the secrets that were slowly suffocating me.

By August 6, 2023, the urgency of the situation had hardened my resolve. I decided to start by carefully documenting and gathering evidence from my home and office. Every small detail now seemed crucial as I tried to piece together the puzzle that had taken over my life.

During this relentless search for clarity, I discovered someone with very deep pockets was involved in the bounty hunt against me. The reach of this mystery extended further than I could have imagined, and included very powerful entities with significant influence.

As the shadows grew darker, so did my determination to unravel the mysteries surrounding me. This brought me closer to the heart of a conspiracy that seemed beyond reason.

August 7, 2023: The Battle for My Sanctuary

August 7, 2023, marked the start of a terrifying chapter as Peter Pottinger's plot continued to unfold. My once-peaceful porch became a battleground, and I constantly found myself scrubbing away the remnants of Lucifer Yellow, which my malicious neighbors brazenly threw onto it. What was supposed to be a space for relaxation and reflection had turned into a front line in an invisible war.

My neighbors, unaware pawns in this twisted game, walked by casually, not realizing the chaos they were contributing to. A deep sense of isolation settled in as I scrubbed away the evidence of their unwitting involvement. My porch, which had once been a refuge, was now tainted by the toxic presence of Lucifer Yellow.

The challenges grew as I faced the deliberate targeting of my personal space but also the unintended consequences of Peter Pottinger's actions. His use of irradiated birdseed in this covert warfare added another layer of complexity. Going out to my porch, a place where I once found peace, became a daily struggle between the need for fresh air and the burden of constant cleaning.

Adding to the irony, the Homeowners Association (HOA) had strict rules against bird feeders, a rule that seemed to be ignored in the common area between my building and the neighboring one. Five bird feeders, two of which were owned by Peter Pottinger, hung in plain view, blatantly defying the regulations. The common area, meant to foster a sense of community, had become an example of the larger deception at play. Pottinger's calculated actions, which seemed harmless to those unaware, were casting a shadow over the tranquility that residents deserved.

The battle against the tainted porch and the irradiated birdseed had become a symbol of a larger struggle against the forces working against me. As I dealt with the physical mess and the psychological toll, the need to understand the motives behind these acts grew stronger. The porch, now a contested space, became a symbol of resilience and defiance in the face of organized chaos. With each scrub, I was determined to cleanse not just the surface but to uncover the truth buried beneath the layers of deception. The battle was just beginning, and the porch would be the frontline in my quest for justice and peace.

As August unfolded, I became more determined to reclaim my porch. My plan was to repaint and seal the light fixture, but this seemingly simple task quickly turned into a maze of challenges.

The first problem was the malfunctioning outlets, a puzzle that brought several electricians to my door. The power surge caused by Peter Pottinger had thrown my electrical system into disarray. Determined to fix it, I began the process of troubleshooting and replacing old fixtures with sturdy, old-fashioned alternatives. I started recording videos of the garage and the exterior of each building where new black wires – wires that hadn't been there before – were now visible. According to the HOA, these wires should have been hidden to match the building's interior and exterior, but it seemed people had gotten lazy.

Samuel Owen, in one of his cryptic moments, had once advised me to "tighten the screws." This advice now took on a strange significance, as if it held the key to stabilizing the unraveling threads of my reality. It felt like a warning, hinting at the turmoil ahead and would test my resilience and resourcefulness.

Undeterred, I set out to revamp my porch. But the project escalated when the light fixture, once a warm and welcoming feature, became a source of the inexplicable. A surge of freezing air began seeping through the space between the drywall and the recessed lighting fixture, a reminder of the unseen forces at play.

My frustration rose as I tried to seal the intrusion with spray foam – a seemingly simple solution that spiraled into chaos. The foam, stubborn and defiant, refused to set, leaving me with a sticky, uncontrollable substance that mirrored the chaos invading my life.

In a fit of anger and desperation, I kept spraying the foam, unaware of the consequences that would follow. The sticky substance clung to my hands, and the stubborn residue wouldn't come off for months until September, when I moved into my new apartment and finally sealed it with a liquid bandage – a symbolic act of closure.

The "nitrogen-cold " air and the stubborn foam became metaphors for the chilling reality I was facing. With each layer of chaos, the porch bore witness to the unraveling of normalcy, reflecting the cracks in my life.

Having worked hard to restore my porch to some sense of normalcy, I sought comfort in the familiar aisles of TJ Maxx in Sugar House, eager to add some life to my space with decorative items. Little did I know that the illusion of normalcy would continue to unravel in unexpected ways.

As I wandered through the aisles, the atmosphere in TJ Maxx felt different, as if an invisible force was at work. The people around me acted in ways that suggested a coordinated effort to push me into submission. A woman, perhaps unknowingly part of this plot, placed a lotion bottle on display with the words "Just relax" on it. I couldn't help but scoff at the irony, recognizing the hidden messages that seemed to infiltrate every part of my life.

Undeterred, I continued shopping, determined to find items that would add a personal touch to my carefully curated porch. Among my purchases were white wood sticks, chosen for their aesthetic appeal and as a strategic deterrent against the unseen electromagnetic warfare that had become an unwelcome part of my life.

On August 7th, I set about spray-painting the wooden sticks black, a task that quickly presented unexpected challenges. The matte black paint, which I had hoped would blend seamlessly with the porch's aesthetic, defied my efforts by turning into a glossy sheen. The paint, like the forces I was fighting, had a deceptive quality, casting an unintended shine that did not align with my vision for the project.

The struggle went beyond just the paint, revealing a pattern of interference whenever I tried to improve my porch. It became clear that leaving any project unfinished was an open invitation for external tampering. The masterminds, who seemed determined to prevent me from completing anything, left their mark by tampering with the paint and adding another chemical component that made the process even more difficult.

The unsettling realization hit me – finishing projects was actively discouraged, a belief rooted in something Samuel had once shared with me: that addicts rarely start and finish tasks. Every stroke of paint on the porch carried the weight of resistance. The shiny black wood sticks, a symbol of defiance, stood in stark contrast to the forces working tirelessly to stop me from finishing anything.

My porch revealed the challenges I was facing. Even trying to paint it turned into an act of resistance against constant interference.

CHAPTER SIX

DETERMINED

As the hidden forces continued, August 8, 2023, brought a new wave of challenges. Determined to document the incessant electromagnetic interference in my life, I recorded the screens in my car, capturing the disruptions that had become all too familiar. I didn't expect this day to tie into a larger narrative, revealing a strange incident that had rocked the Sugar House area.

A message from Kirk, a neighbor in our building's group chat, revealed something startling – a crane had struck multiple power lines, leaving nearly 12,000 people without power.

The incident took place near an old power plant that had recently been revived and rebranded as "The Power Plant." This revelation was unsettling; the power lines now fed into this once-abandoned site, bringing it back to life as an operational facility.

Adding to the strangeness, Kirk and Shanna, other neighbors in the chat, jokingly declared themselves as part of "Team KimiKat," not realizing that KimiKat was actually a made up name I gave myself for the web of relationships within our building.

That same day, Pier, another neighbor with knowledge about radiation, shared a chilling update: a semi-truck had caught fire near the power plant on I-80, and he warned everyone to avoid inhaling the smoke.

Shanna responded, noting the irony of just having opened their windows on what seemed like a nice summer night. The oddness of anyone opening windows in the middle of August only added to the surreal unfolding events.

In my ongoing battle against the invisible forces affecting my life, I tried a new approach. On August 8th, I added copper plant spirals around my porch, strategically placing them around the decorative wood sticks. These spirals were meant to act as magnetic deterrents, symbols of my fight against relentless interference.

By August 9th, my focus turned to "Big Daddy," the towering pine tree near my condo. Somebody had finally groomed it, but its branches still carried the weight of metallic dust -a reminder of the covert actions affecting even the natural elements around me.

Resilience Amidst Deceit

On August 11th, I decided to take action once again. Armed with copper wire I'd bought from Amazon, I carefully wrapped it around the wrought iron balcony on my porch, creating a makeshift shield against the overwhelming magnetic energy that had invaded my space – a physical defense against the unseen forces working against me.

In a desperate attempt to maintain peace, I reached out to my neighbors, asking them to lower the humming noise that had become an ever-present reminder of the chaos around me. My requests were met with the usual silence as my neighbors continued their lives, seemingly unaware of the unrest echoing through the building.

Meanwhile, Peter Pottinger, the relentless antagonist in this story, continued his malicious acts. Lucifer Yellow kept pouring down my drain spout, mirroring the dark conspiracy at play. What was once just a simple drain spout had now become a channel for the toxic intentions slowly destroying my home's peace.

Despite my best efforts to fortify the porch and shield it from the magnetic onslaught, the humming persisted as a constant reminder of the unseen forces that refused to let me find peace. The porch, now covered in copper wire and symbols of defiance stood as a testament to my resilience in the face of deceit.

As the days blurred together, my porch became another battleground between personal defiance and relentless external interference. It seemed like they had turned my entire life into a warscape. The struggle for normalcy became a complicated dance, where every step forward was met with an unseen force pushing back, testing my limits. The porch became a small-scale version of the larger battle – a space where visible and invisible forces clashed in a chaotic symphony. Each passing day deepened the story, leaving me to navigate the complex mix of truth and lies, resilience and surrender, in my quest to restore peace.

Lifting the Digital Veil

August 13, 2023, began with a search for answers, leading me deep into the digital world in pursuit of the truths that keep evading me. Confronted with ransomware and unable to rely on the help of my best friend – a companion of two decades – I dived into the online realm, hoping to find some clarity.

I navigated to whois.gandi.net, hoping it would reveal something about the mysterious web address that had been haunting me. What I found was both intriguing and confusing: a private address hidden behind layers of digital secrecy. The site had been created on February 10, 2020, well before the chaos in my life had begun to spiral out of control.

To my surprise, I discovered that I was listed as the site's owner, administrator, and technical contact. This seemed to suggest that I was the one controlling this digital mystery, yet there was a twist – a corporate entity based in Minneapolis, Minnesota, was listed as the billing contact. This mix of personal ownership and corporate involvement added another layer of complexity. External server names like ns-5-a.gandi.net, ns-41-b.gandi.net, and ns-148-c.gandi.net hovered in the digital background, hinting at connections beyond my understanding.

The date, "February 10, 2024," loomed on the horizon, adding a sense of urgency to my investigation. The digital entity I had uncovered was set to expire on August 25, 2023, unless something changed. The countdown in the digital world mirrored the impending sense of change in my physical surroundings.

At 11:57, I posted a meme on Instagram that read, "Bringing down billionaires - coming soon by KimiKat." The digital world became my outlet for expressing the need to unravel the tangled web of secrets that had ensnared my life.

As the lines between the digital and physical worlds blurred, my search for answers took on new significance. The digital veil, while revealing bits of information, resisted full disclosure. My journey into the depths of technology had only just begun, with the promise of shedding light on the shadows that extended far beyond my porch and into the digital world.

CHAPTER SEVEN

THE ILLUSION OF NORMALCY

A Descent into Darkness

August 18, 2023, marked a disturbing chapter in my life. The day began with a deceptive type of peacefulness as I sought relief by the pool, trying to lessen the weight of all the trauma. The poolside offered a momentary break, the water was refreshing, but an undercurrent of unease whispered that tranquility was merely an illusion, with unseen shadows preparing to disrupt the fragile calm.

After a short swim, I moved to bask in the sun, sipping on a half-filled glass of champagne in my attempt to find a moment of peace. As time slipped away and I prepared to leave, an inexplicable compulsion led me to pull a power switch on one of the buildings by the pool.

In that disorienting moment, a sense of urgency overwhelmed me - a need to save others from directed energy warfare. This impulse transcended rational thought as I pulled the switch a cascade of events unfolded with unsettling speed. Outside the clubhouse, the police awaited my like phantoms. An officer's casual inquiry about my age carried an undertone of surprise, but before I could fully grasp the situation, I was handcuffed and confined within the police car.

The Dance Continues: Blurred Lines Between Time and Place

The disorienting dance between reality and mystery intensified in the murky interior of the Salt Lake County Jail. My booking sheet painted a distorted picture – a narrative that defied logic and blurred the lines between time and place.

The date and time of my arrest were listed as 8/18/2023 at 18:33, with the arrest location pointing to the residence of Jake Nuton, the HOA president. The booking date and time, 8/18/2023 at 22:14, felt oddly disconnected, pulling me into a moment where time itself seemed to lose its usual order, unraveling like a tangled thread.

My time in holding was brief, with only three of us: myself, an African American kid, and the unexpected arrival of Trevor. The prisoner property sheet claimed I possessed a damaged cell phone which was a blatant lie. The absence of my signature on the intake form, the false allegation of intoxication, and the denial of the right to make three calls highlighted the confusing nature of my predicament.

Stripped of autonomy, I was given pants and subjected to a DNA swab before leaving the jail. They forced me to sleep sitting up due to an unspoken jail rule that made reclining forbidden.

Amidst the enforced stillness, a voice cut through the monotony – Dan, a transferee from an Oregon prison. His unbelievable journey to the Salt Lake County Jail mirrored the trajectory of my own circumstances.

A choice lay before me – compliance or defiance. The phrase *"Let's see which way the motherfucking wind is blowing today!"* became a guiding mantra as I navigated the unpredictable currents. I observed Dan's actions and noticed a well-dressed figure to the right; his body language gave off a silent warning – DON'T DO THAT. He was a man caught in altercations with his roommate, exuding an air of authority that could have been an anchor in the stormy sea of the C.T.A. (Community Therapeutic Approach) nightmare. In hindsight, the missed opportunity to connect became a reminder of the intricate alliances that wove the fabric of survival within the jail.

As the dance of alliances and uncertainties continued, the Salt Lake County Jail emerged as the intersection point where the shadows of the past intertwined with the mystery of the present. The journey through the maze of the C.T.A. nightmare became a relentless pursuit of truth amid the warped echoes of reality, each step forward revealing new layers of the complex dance that bound me to unseen forces.

Whispers of Betrayal

As the gears of the Salt Lake County Jail shifted, propelling me toward an impending release, an unexpected encounter added intrigue to my growing narrative —eated beside me was a woman employed in the same building as my company, Gateway Title. She was a hospice worker arrested for tampering with her neighbor's Amazon packages – an experience that eerily mirrored my own with parcel interference.

Despite her attempts at friendliness, a silent vow echoed within me – I would never be her friend. Yet, the twisted dance of survival forced a fake of connection to hide my true intentions

Nausea gripped me as I navigated the jail's maze. Seeking assistance led me to the nurses' station, where they offered me a protein shake in response to my plea. In a moment of vulnerability, I disclosed my exposure to Lucifer Yellow and the possible installation of eye implants. The female officers' disdainful glances and the nurses' indifferent shrugs underscored the isolation within the jail's crucible.

Summoning strength, I returned to the holding area, where a screen displayed a help number for reporting sexual abuse. I made a calculated decision, diverging from the expected course – I left a message about a more ominous reality. The community's therapeutic interventionist, Peter Pottinger, and his use of Lucifer Yellow and electromagnetic warfare against me became the focal point of my disclosure.

Another call followed, unveiling a web of conspiracy involving prominent figures. In a whispered revelation, I left a message exposing the alleged machinations of Loki, my parents, and the evasive upper class orchestrating a covert plot to eliminate the community in pursuit of their "Smart City" agenda.

The whispers of betrayal echoed through the walls of the jail. As the situation grew more complex, I worked harder to uncover the lies, exposing a story filled with betrayal and hidden agendas. With each discovery, I found myself drawn further into the unsettling reality of the C.T.A. ordeal.

Defying the Facade

My journey through the legal system took an unexpected turn when I was sent to Jordan Valley South for a required medical examination. Hoping to speed up my release, I agreed to the exam, presenting it as a cooperative step in the process.

Transported by the Sheriff's Office, the trip felt strangely distant – one male officer, one female officer, and the anticipation of the upcoming examination. When we arrived, I insisted on having a female present during the examination. The female officer, calm and composed, stayed by my side.

The doctor called to perform the examination had an unsettling attitude, with a grin that suggested an inappropriate eagerness. He mentioned that a pelvic exam would be part of the procedure. Feeling a strong sense of defiance, I held his gaze firmly, refusing to back down.

"You're not doing a physical examination on me," I declared, refusing to submit to the invasive procedure. I asserted my belief that I had endured sexual assault. The doctor's initial enthusiasm shifted to shock at my statement, and his defensive reaction revealed a hint of guilt.

Despite his objections, I held my ground and asserted my right to refuse consent. My refusal became a way to protect myself from any further harm. "The fact that you are getting defensive is even more reason for me not to have you do the physical exam," I said, pointing out the inconsistency in his response.

This encounter marked an important moment – a stand against the violation of personal boundaries within a system that seemed increasingly unclear. As I continued to fight for my autonomy, each act of resistance demonstrated the strength I had developed through the challenges of the C.T.A. ordeal. I faced each step of the process with determination, refusing to let anything take away my sense of control.

Whispers Behind Bars

Back at the county jail, I found myself in a room with two disparate companions – a woman yearning for her husband and an addict sprawled across a bench, claiming her territory. I stood, uncomfortably aware of the intense emotions filling the small room.

As I looked around, I noticed something unusual. People wearing FBI uniforms entered the facility and headed toward the computers near the holding cells. The scene raised questions and left me wondering what was happening.

In the midst of the chaos, a silent exchange took place between the people in the room and me. Through small but meaningful gestures, they signaled for me to move my head in a certain way – similar to setting up facial recognition on a phone. I followed their instructions, unsure of what it meant.

The fragile connection was suddenly broken when someone appeared in front of my cell. Trevor, or whatever name he was going by, made his point clear. He pulled a hair tie from his hair, ran his hands down his arms, and tapped his nose – a signal telling me to stop what I was doing immediately.

My encounter with Trevor, the inmate I first met in holding, was brief but carried an unspoken sense of warning. The Overcrowded Release sheet, which seemed unimportant at first, contained a glaring mistake – my middle name was listed as "Joe" instead of "Jo." This small but important error reflected a system where details were often wrong, and identities could easily become unclear.

Outside the bars, hidden activities continued. Errors in official records and silent signals from unknown figures suggested a hidden reality. As I tried to make sense of the C.T.A. ordeal, the quiet exchanges in the jail revealed layers of secrecy, each interaction hinting at the truths buried within the system.

Echoes of Coercion

August 19, 2023, began with conflicting emotions. After being released from the county jail, a male officer, showing little concern, warned me that I had limited time to call about my DNA and address my case, or I could be arrested again.

With just my keys and phone, I stepped back into the world. I quickly realized I couldn't afford public transportation, so I walked home. The walk was exhausting as I tried to process everything that had happened.

As I walked, the pressure of everything weighed on me. My phone, which had been my connection to the world, now felt like a burden. I left it behind in a planter outside a pawn shop. It was a strange act, driven by forces I didn't fully grasp.

When I finally got home, all I wanted was to wash away the experience. Taking a shower felt necessary, like a way to cleanse myself from the time I spent in jail. Following Samuel's advice, I carefully sealed my clothes, preserving them as potential evidence of what I'd been through.

The day left me feeling torn between freedom and control, strength and vulnerability. Every step I took was a way to regain some sense of control in a world that felt increasingly out of my hands.

Shadows of Allegation

August 20, 2023, is a day I won't soon forget. What started as a simple task of getting a bicycle turned into a surreal experience. It became a pivotal moment when the line between reality and nightmare blurred. I was left to confront not only external threats but also the disturbing realization that the forces manipulating my life were far more sinister than I had imagined.

As I walked down an alley, I saw a garage filled with items that looked like my sister's belongings. Lost in thought, I stood there, unsure of what to do. Suddenly, a woman started yelling at me, accusing me of things I hadn't done. Her husband, who must have been at least 6'2", ran toward me grabbing my head and slapping me hard across the face. In the struggle to get away, I lost my sunglasses and ran down a nearby side street.

At that moment, a Salt Lake City Police car appeared. I flagged it down, out of breath, and explained what had happened, asking the officers to help me press charges. They went to the house, but when they returned, their response surprised me. They said I was the one "not acting right" and that the man had the right to protect his property.

Shortly after the altercation in the alley the situation worsened. After the assault, an ambulance was called, leading to my involuntary admission to St. Mark's Hospital. I was detained for hours, with my attempts to leave met with force. The ordeal escalated when a nurse mentioned something about a "pink slip[10]," a term I didn't understand. Moments later, the nurse changed his wording to "blue slip," leaving me more confused than ever. This shifting narrative left me feeling lost and unsure of what was real.

Things took an even darker turn when I was transferred against my will to Lakeview Behavioral, where I was confined for another 24 hours. The invasive nature of this experience included an MRI scan which I didn't even ask for, but they did it anyway. When they got the results back they reported to me, describing my brain as "immaculate." I'm sure they're looking for evidence to say that I was a drug user, suffering from a psychotic break, and we're quite disappointed to find neither was the case.

---

10. Pink sheets/slips are emergency applications for involuntary commitment without certification form completed by a peace officer or mental health officer requesting temporary commitment of a person. Blue sheet is an emergency application for involuntary commitment with certification form completed by a responsible person and certified by a licensed physician or designated examiner requesting temporary commitment of a person. When these slips are issues, it can cause professionals to have a stigma towards an individual because they are primarily used for those who are mentally ill, or displaying signs of being a danger to themselves or others. In Kimberly's case, she was neither mentally ill or a danger to anyone, but treated as such until the forced evaluations exonerated her.

Later, when I looked at the records from St. Mark's and Lakeview Behavioral Health, it was clear that the system didn't fully understand what was going on. The accusations were confusing and hard to make sense of, adding another layer of mystery to everything that had happened.

Shadows Persist

August 21, 2023, was a day marked by many desperate choices for my survival. Fearing for my life, I made the difficult decision to sell my condo and find refuge in a new place – the Brickyard apartment complex down the street. This drastic move was a chilling memory of a Twitter post in which I had declared my autonomy over my health rights, challenging the powers of Loki, the World Health Organization (WHO), and the World Economic Forum (WEF).

August 22, 2023, unfolded as another day of distress. A sense of impending doom drove me to Walmart, where I found myself compelled to perform strange movements – an eerie dance that had been shown to me repeatedly by those 'pulling the strings' games I never agreed to play.

In the makeup aisle, I struggled against the invisible forces controlling my actions. It felt like a cruel spectacle, with the people around me unknowingly participating in my torment. They tried to guide me through the same movements Samuel Owen had demonstrated during our encounters – echoes of the choreography Dan had imposed on me at the county jail. Determined to uncover the truth, I contacted my attorney and private investigator, urging them to obtain the Walmart video and investigate the footage from the county jail and St. Mark's Hospital.

As I continued to experience strange encounters with the shadows surrounding me, the pursuit of evidence became my only hope. In a reality where every action seemed orchestrated by unseen forces, I was trapped in a web of manipulation and uncertainty, desperately trying to regain control of my life.

CHAPTER EIGHT

UNSEEN FORCES

September 1, 2023, brought an unexpected revelation, trapping me in a legal situation created by my parents. The day started with the harsh realization that I had missed an important hearing about my treatment and intervention. My parents had arranged the hearing without telling me, making sure I didn't know I was supposed to be there.

In my inbox, an email from Sandy Keys, my parents' attorney, caught my attention. As I opened the message, I began to understand the seriousness of the situation. Sandy Keys, a new person in this already complicated situation, emphasized how urgent the matter was.

"Good morning, Kim," the email began, formal and detached. "I am Sandy Keys, and I'm assisting on the attached case. I'm emailing you these documents so that you have the information you need to participate in this case."

The email included documents full of legal terms and instructions about the hearing I was supposed to attend. The courtroom at 501 Chipeta Way, Salt Lake City, Utah, was set to be the setting for the next chapter of my life. The date, Friday, September 8th, 2023, at 9:00 AM, felt like it was quickly approaching.

The challenges didn't end with the upcoming court hearing. I was also required to undergo two mandatory examinations before the hearing, further invading my autonomy. The locations listed, Huntsman Behavioral Health of Salt Lake City or the Huntsman Mental Health Institute/Hospital, were places where I would be examined and judged by others.

The pressure in the email was obvious – the legal process was already underway, and I found myself trapped in a situation I hadn't created. The lack of control and the secrecy of the process reflected the larger pattern of interference and control that had come to dominate my life.

As the sun set on September 1st, I came to terms with the fact that my path was heading toward an uncertain legal battle. The upcoming hearings, examinations, and the influence of my family all felt like a heavy burden.

Facing this unexpected legal situation, I found myself at a crossroads, unsure of how to defend myself. Surrounded by outside interference, the path ahead required strength and focus as I dealt with the forces trying to control my future.

A Legal Encounter

September 8, 2023, was the day I entered the Huntsman Mental Health Institute for a hearing that would uncover unexpected challenges. The atmosphere was tense as I faced the uncertainty. I was taken to a waiting room, where my mother tried to greet me warmly, but I remained silent as I sat down.

A woman in her thirties, sitting in the waiting room with me, broke the tension by asking about her appearance. Concerned about how she looked for the hearing, she asked if she seemed presentable. I commented on the matching hospital-issued socks and shirt, and we shared a brief connection. She offered me a piece of gum, which I accepted, and then she offered it to another patient, who declined.

An acquaintance of the woman I was sitting with arrived, starting a conversation about their mutual friend's meth use and recent incarceration. Meanwhile, my mother became more impatient and asked the officer about the delay, and I could feel the weight of being watched.

The room where the judge waited felt very formal. The judge, assuming the reason for my presence, asked if my case was about substance abuse rather than mental health. My uncertain response led to another question about legal representation. Even though my repeated requests for an attorney had been denied, the judge decided to extend the case by two weeks, advising me to prepare and find legal counsel.

Douglas Grant from Legal Shield was recommended by a colleague I had worked with earlier that year as an ambassador for the local Chamber of Commerce. As things unfolded, I began to navigate the legal process, finding a path that required both strength and understanding.

A Crucible of Evaluations

After the hearing, I was left trying to deal with the growing intervention in my life, armed only with a list of treatment providers to help me navigate the confusing situation I had been placed in.

The names on the list seemed important, as if they were central to the situation my parents had started. With a tight deadline looming – two weeks or ten business days – I had to arrange two essential treatment evaluations. Determined to keep some control over my life, I set out to contact all four providers.

The first name on the list was Dr. Seoul Sebastian. Wanting to take control, I called Dr. Sebastian, only to be told I needed to pay a $4,000 retainer. Although I was hesitant, I understood the importance of protecting my freedom from involuntary commitment and decided to agree.

The second provider, Stephanie Carr, recommended by Sandy Keys, led to an uncomfortable visit in Draper, UT. The office felt off, with random water bottles placed around as if for hidden recording. Feeling uneasy, I declined the offer for an eight-to-ten-hour evaluation, explaining that I had responsibilities running a business.

Despite these setbacks and sensing something was off, I reached out to my long-time therapist, Jared. Our five-year relationship built on trust felt like a lifeline in the midst of everything. However, I was surprised when Jared handed the evaluation over to one of his employees, a therapist who was probably in his mid-twenties.

The evaluation, which was supposed to support my case, took a concerning turn. The young therapist's report portrayed me as abrupt and defensive – a narrative that clashed with my own perception of the interaction. The differences between my experience and the therapist's account left me questioning the true motives behind the evaluation.

As the evaluation reports came in, I found myself caught between conflicting narratives. Instead of clarifying my mental state, the evaluations seemed to be used by outside forces. What should have been a way to understand my situation turned into a struggle for my autonomy, where my words and experiences were shaped by others' agendas.

The next chapter of my journey was set to reveal more of this intervention, with the evaluations acting as both a shield and a weapon in my continued fight for self-determination and control over my future.

CHAPTER NINE

SHADOWS OF DECEIT

On September 12, 2023, my experience with coercive control took another turn when I ended up at Duffy's Tavern. What started as an ordinary evening, after touring a new apartment complex, turned into an unexpected encounter with Trevor.

As we sat down to a simple dinner of pizza, our conversation turned to people like Peter Pottinger, caught in the web of coercion. Trevor, who seemed knowledgeable about secrecy, shared tips on how to protect privacy in a world of constant surveillance. He recommended using a burner phone, a Faraday bag, and public wifi – practical advice for keeping information private in an era where it's hard to do so.

After dinner, I invited Trevor to see my new apartment. As we drove, we made a quick stop for fuel, where Trevor suggested taking the I-80 route. I agreed, and we set off down the highway.

As we drove along I-80, I suddenly became disoriented. Familiar landmarks looked distorted, and before I knew it, we had taken an unexpected exit onto 33rd South, heading east. The atmosphere around us changed quickly, not because of anything natural, but because it felt like something was manipulating the environment – a man-made thunderstorm seemed to appear out of nowhere.

Metal plates lined the road, and power lines hung low, creating an unsafe and unsettling scene. It was clear that this wasn't an ordinary storm. It seemed like a deliberate setup, part of a larger effort to intimidate and distract me. The storm felt like an attempt to throw me off track and disrupt my plans, showing just how far these controlling forces would go to keep me off balance.

The message was clear: I was being discouraged from bringing Trevor back to my apartment. The pressure I was facing wasn't just mental – it was affecting the world around me. Every move seemed like part of a larger effort to control me, where each action was meant to provoke a response and keep me trapped.

When we finally arrived at my apartment, the storm still weighed on my mind. Despite everything that had happened, Trevor calmly made his way through the secure side door to the garage, as if he had expected the strange turn of events all along.

As we moved through the apartment, Trevor made some odd comments. He mentioned the pendant lights above my bar and said he wanted to get similar ones, which was strange since his last known place was an apartment. He also recognized a leaf blower I had bought to clear chemical residue from my porch, which made me uneasy. It felt like something foreign, like the presence of Lucifer Yellow, had started to affect both the outside and personal spaces of my new apartment.

When Trevor asked to use my restroom, it reminded me of past invasions of privacy, like the wine party where people used contact tracing as an excuse to enter my home. As Trevor opened the freezer, he gave a quick glance that made me wonder if he was suggesting I store something there – another clue that added to the mystery surrounding him.

Throughout the evening, Trevor asked about different parts of my life – micro-dosing, my pole classes, and recent trips to Montana. His questions showed he knew more than I expected, making me wonder if his visit was more than just a coincidence.

As the night went on and we eventually moved to the bedroom, the boundaries between intimacy and coercion began to blur. The room felt heavy with unspoken truths, becoming both a place of comfort and a setting for the unpredictable events unfolding in my life.

When Trevor left, his casual question about the elevator route to the garage and his comment about the "appliance graveyard" – referring to the odd collection of discarded appliances in the garage – stuck with me. The encounter left me wondering about Trevor's real role and how deeply these manipulations had infiltrated my personal life.

The journey through coercive control continued, with each step uncovering more deception. I found myself constantly searching for the truth in a reality that felt more like a carefully constructed simulation than the life I once knew.

CHAPTER TEN

WEB OF ALLEGIANCES

On September 15, 2023, my journey through coercive control took me into the local Chamber of Commerce's referral community. At a luncheon, I met Kat, a representative from LegalShield, whose advice became a key support in the legal confusion surrounding me. Kat and I had worked together as ambassadors for the Chamber of Commerce, and this connection offered a sense of reassurance during such chaotic times. She recommended I download the LegalShield app and submit any issues I faced so they could be quickly assigned to an attorney.

Through this connection, I was introduced to Douglas Grant, the attorney who would defend me against my parents' petition. The trust I had built with Kat over our six months of working together added an extra layer of comfort, helping me feel more secure during this difficult time.

During the luncheon, a mysterious concept was introduced to me – the idea of being a target within a 10.5-mile radius. It seemed vague and unclear at the time, leaving me unsure of its true meaning or relevance.

The full weight of this revelation hit me during a phone conversation with my aunt and uncle on September 29th. Their words struck me with the force of a thunderbolt: my condo was located at the exact center of a map outlining one of the current Smart City proposals. What had once seemed like a neutral term now carried ominous connotations. I realized that the 10.5-mile radius wasn't just a random measurement – it marked the boundaries of a Smart City, a concept that began to feel far darker, almost like a concentration camp.

The narrative took an unexpected turn as these pieces of information fell into place. The Smart City proposal, which I had initially brushed off, began to reveal its true implications. The tangled web of legal counsel, alliances, and newfound awareness grew more complex, forcing me to face the looming shadows of this Smart City – a new dimension of the coercive control that had taken over my life. The journey unfolded further, peeling back layers of deception and drawing me closer to a truth I was both desperate to understand and fearful of discovering.

Battlegrounds of Business

On September 19, 2023, the focus shifted to my business. Faced with the looming threat of a hostile takeover orchestrated by my own children, I enlisted the help of an IT company to fortify the defenses of my office server and computer. Protecting the core of my professional life had become a top priority, pushing me to take proactive steps to safeguard everything I had built.

With their technological expertise, the IT firm arrived as defenders of my digital world. Their mission was simple yet critical: to strengthen the security of my office server and personal computer, making them secure against any attempts to take control. In this battle of power dynamics, the business environment became a high-stakes arena where every decision had the potential to shift the balance.

As the IT team set up the necessary safeguards, I found myself facing two battles: one against the digital risks that could jeopardize my business and another against the familial pressures that threatened its survival. The fight against coercive control grew more complex, extending beyond personal struggles to encompass the need to protect my professional independence.

This part of my journey became a deeper dive into the clash between personal and professional power struggles. The business world turned into a battleground where family interests and my career collided. Bringing in the IT firm wasn't just about protecting my data – it was a deliberate effort to stay ahead, recognizing that my fight for independence touched every aspect of my life, including the foundation of my livelihood.

By the end of September 19, 2023, the lines between my personal and professional battles had blurred. Each step I took to protect my business reflected the larger struggle against the forces encroaching on my independence. Balancing family conflict with the urgent need to secure my livelihood, I faced a growing challenge that demanded both careful strategy and unwavering resolve.

Shadows on the Lens

On September 21, 2023, I took a step toward rebuilding normalcy with a visit to a local real estate office. Kristy, my employee, joined me as we had our headshots taken by the marketing director. The session marked a small but important step forward – creating new business cards, something I had postponed for too long while isolating myself in my condo to guard against outside threats.

The headshots symbolized more than a business update—they were an attempt to hold onto a semblance of normalcy amid the turmoil. As the camera shutter snapped, capturing our images, I couldn't ignore the unease that came with creating another visual record. Recent efforts to fortify my digital defenses against the looming threat of a hostile takeover by my children had made me hyper-aware of the vulnerabilities even small actions could introduce.

That evening, I returned to pole class after a long break, seeking a different kind of strength. For me, pole dancing wasn't just about fitness – it was my outlet, combining exercise, stress relief, and emotional grounding. The pole became a way to reclaim some sense of control, providing a temporary escape from the overwhelming complexities of the coercion that had seeped into every corner of my life.

During the class, Trevor's earlier questions about micro-dosing and pole dancing crept back into my mind, their once-innocent tone now feeling unsettling. Reflecting on his visit to my apartment earlier that month, I couldn't ignore the weight of his comments. His mention of the freezer and the cryptic suggestion to store evidence there added an ominous layer to our interactions, leaving me questioning his motives and the true nature of our connection.

As I moved through the pole routines, I realized that reclaiming my sense of strength and control was an ongoing process, even during moments of doubt. Balancing the demands of rebuilding my professional life, navigating unseen manipulations, and carving out spaces for personal empowerment created a dynamic, challenging path forward. Each spin on the pole was a small act of defiance and a reminder of my capacity to adapt and persevere.

CHAPTER ELEVEN

THE DANCE OF SHADOWS

On September 28, 2023, my journey reached a turning point, weaving together moments of strength and uncertainty. That evening, I attended a pole class – a place where I could focus on myself, finding a balance between resilience and the challenges that lingered. Each movement around the pole reminded me of my determination to reclaim control, even as I navigated a world clouded by doubt and mistrust.

In the dimly lit studio, Riri, a familiar face from the wine party, stood out among the others. Her role in the invasive contact tracing from that gathering lingered in my mind, adding layers of complexity to her presence. Now, wearing a mask, she seemed to carry an unspoken message – perhaps a subtle reminder that even within the sanctuary of my new space, secrecy was necessary for protection.

Riri's subdued demeanor suggested she was burdened by guilt, a silent acknowledgment of her part in those earlier invasive acts. The unspoken tension in the studio mirrored the complexity of my situation, where every interaction seemed layered with hidden motives. The pole, once a source of strength and liberation, now stood as a quiet observer to the delicate balance between trust and betrayal unfolding around me.

As this chapter came to a close, Riri's masked presence in the pole studio felt like a symbol of the hidden layers within her involvement in the covert forces at play. Her actions echoed the complexities of the manipulations surrounding me, and the dance of shadows continued. Each movement, each interaction, felt like part of a larger, intricate choreography of coercion that had subtly shaped my life.

This chapter brought me to a crossroads of trust, suspicion, vulnerability, and strength. The pole, with its silent grace, became a symbol of resilience, reminding me that even in the shadows, the pursuit of empowerment continues. As the chapter closed, the echoes of spins and masked glances lingered, setting the stage for the next act in a journey shaped by the unseen forces of coercive control.

Veil Lifted

As September 30, 2023, arrived, the final chapters of my journey through coercive control began to unfold. The weight of revelation pressed heavily upon me, and with each item I unpacked, a subtle horror emerged – tampered possessions ordered from Temu, intrusions that stretched far beyond the boundaries of my former home. My furniture was adorned with countless stickers, stark reminders of the violation of my personal space, proof that the shadows of coercion had crept into even the most mundane parts of my life.

The echoes of manipulated Amazon packages lingered, a constant reminder of a force that wouldn't loosen its grip. But I refused to be deterred. I took a stand by changing the names on my packages, a strategic move designed to confuse those intent on invading my belongings. These calculated acts of resistance marked the closing chapter of a tumultuous journey, a final push toward reclaiming control in the face of relentless manipulation.

This narrative unfolded like a symphony of resilience, woven through personal and professional battles. From the protective confines of my condo to the uncertainties of a new apartment, each step was shadowed by the constant presence of coercive control. As I unpacked the last remnants of the past, the weight of the journey settled in – a testament to the unwavering spirit that endured amidst the shadows.

This odyssey had been one of revelation, where trust became a rare commodity, and alliances were formed with threads of suspicion. The pole, my refuge, stood as a symbol of strength, a silent witness to the complex dance of empowerment amidst the constant shadows.

As October arrived, my journey through the shadows pressed on, uncovering new layers of resistance and adaptation. The echoes of tampered belongings and sticker-covered furniture trailed me into my new apartment, serving as a reminder of the coercive forces that continued to linger at the edges of my life.

But I remained undeterred. I dug deeper into the complexities of this ongoing struggle, committed to reshaping the narrative. Amazon packages, once symbols of vulnerability, turned into a battleground where I used strategic moves to thwart those trying to tamper with my things. Changing the names on the packages was a small but powerful act of defiance – a minor victory in the larger fight against the shadows creeping into my life.

This chapter went beyond the physical, diving into the psychological space where trust had become rare. The dance of resilience went on, driven by the unyielding spirit that had guided me through the maze of coercive control.

As the story unfolded, it became clear that the journey wasn't a straight line but a recurring cycle of finding empowerment in the face of adversity.

The pole, standing firm in the studio, remained a steady companion – symbolizing strength and offering a refuge in the midst of chaos.

October marked the beginning of a new phase, and the upcoming chapters would reveal whether the shadows would grow stronger or if my resilient spirit would finally break free. The journey went on, and with each step, I stayed focused on uncovering the truth, determined to expose the shadows that had come to shape my story.

The Maze of Evaluation

As October began, the complexities of my journey through coercion deepened, weaving together the challenges of court-ordered assessments and the persistent shadows that seemed to follow me. On October 10, 2023, my days were filled with coordinating with Jared, the therapist my parents had chosen for the second critical treatment evaluation.

The original therapist, part of Jared's practice, fell ill at the last moment, and fate intervened to assign another therapist to carry out the court-ordered evaluation. As Jared explained, this process was far more than just a simple assessment – it involved multiple meetings, psychological tests, and outreach to family, friends, and employers to gather collateral sources. The end result would be a detailed evaluation, carefully crafted to meet the court's rigorous standards.

In the complex web of coercion, this assessment became a critical moment where my personal struggles intersected with external evaluations. Jared, overseeing the process, offered insights into the court's exacting standards – a requirement for a thorough assessment that covered both past and present.

Taking advantage of the moment, I requested that Jared clearly state in the evaluation letter that he had been my therapist for the past five years. I also asked for his professional insight into my mental state, hoping he would shed light on the complexities that had shaped our therapeutic relationship.

As the process progressed, the assessment transformed from a simple court-mandated task into a mirror reflecting the complexities of my mental state. With a new therapist now involved, this evaluation had the potential to become a turning point in my journey – a moment where the forces of coercion and my resilience would collide.

Shadows in the Daylight

On October 13, 2023, the shadows of my life continued to loom, despite my growing resilience. At 5:30 in the morning, I woke up to record another video of the persistent waves of Lucifer Yellow emanating from my new apartment. The chemical, carried through the vents, remained a constant, silent adversary in my ongoing battle against covert intrusions.

Later that day, I repainted my porch as an act of defiance against the persistent contamination that no amount of cleaning could remove. Unable to scrub away the lingering effects of coercion, I covered the surfaces with acrylic-based paint, symbolically reclaiming control over my space. The side tables, too resistant to be fully cleansed, underwent the same transformation, shifting from symbols of vulnerability to markers of resilience.

With every new acquisition, my mother's questions about their origins took on a different tone - an unspoken acknowledgment that replacements might be needed. The shoes, just a bit too big, became a symbolic reminder that even the smallest details of my life were open to scrutiny and possible interference.

Needing a break, I turned to a liquid motion class, where I met Mel, one of the studio owners, who would later become a true friend. The class offered a much-needed escape, a space where I could temporarily put aside the physical and emotional weight of coercion.

When I got home, I sat down on my freshly painted porch, only to find the same yellow gas seeping out again. It hit me hard – the covert forces had found their way into my new apartment. Even the smallest choices, like the floor level my apartment manager had offered, seemed to carry more weight than I had realized.

A Tapestry of Interactions

From October 15 to 18, 2023, the story unfolded through a mix of treatment evaluations, birthday celebrations, and legal challenges, each moment adding a new layer to the complex tapestry of my life.

I met with a man in his late twenties at the counseling center for my second treatment evaluation. He asked for brief answers to his questions, and I kept my responses short while he carefully navigated the complexities of my mental state.

Two days after the second evaluation, Jared, the one overseeing the court-mandated assessments, reached out for clarification on my reluctance to involve close family members in the process. I explained that it was a strategic decision to avoid potential biases, and suggested he contact my hairstylist, who had been a steady presence in my life.

On October 18, 2023, my birthday, I decided to attend the Women in Business event hosted by a striking blonde, the chairwoman of the Chamber of Commerce. Thanks to a perk from my office lease, I was able to book a ticket for the event at the conference center. While there, I met Pearl, a photographer, and Sean Smith, a makeup artist. Their excitement about a boudoir session perfectly matched the gift I had planned for myself.

During my birthday celebrations, a message from Prince at LegalShield added another layer of complexity. He was handling my HOA and neighbor stalking case and asked for permission to contact the private detective I had hired for the investigation. The ongoing legal issues had become increasingly intertwined with my everyday life, making it difficult to separate personal matters from the external forces that were shaping my reality.

Returning home, I found a gift waiting for me at the front desk – a gesture from someone I hadn't yet identified. Monte, the new facilities manager, handed it over while also addressing a maintenance request I had made for my sliding glass door trim. The combination of unexpected gifts, legal inquiries, and practical needs further blurred the line between my personal space and the external forces at play, creating a tangled web of events.

A Symphony of Disruption

On October 19, 2023, the disruption persisted, with the lines between my personal space and the external forces closing in. My Wayfair order, meant to protect against electromagnetic interference, arrived in a disappointing condition, tainted and not as expected.

The coffee table I had ordered, meant to serve as a shield against electromagnetic forces, arrived covered in Lucifer Yellow – a stark contrast to the color I had chosen online. This wasn't just a simple visual error; it felt like an invasion, a disruption of my space. Much like the people in my life, the furniture I had selected for comfort was altered, tainted by outside forces.

Undeterred, I set about stripping the table's top, much like I had done with my dining room table in my condo. This wasn't just about restoring its appearance; it was a bold act of reclaiming control – refusing to let the shadows dictate the story of my space.

In a similar turn, the rug and barstools I had bought from a local furniture store also showed signs of tampering before they were delivered. This unsettling discovery reinforced a recurring theme in my life – the constant replacement, a cycle of belongings altered by invisible forces.

Around this time, I discovered something unsettling in my faucets. When I turned them on, expecting clear water in my brand-new apartment, white chunks of material emerged. It was a clear sign of interference in the very infrastructure of my daily life. The lithium salt in the faucets became a symbol of the unseen forces working to disrupt and corrode my sense of stability.

Shadows of Celebration

As October 21, 2023, drew near, the shadows surrounding my life continued to weave their intricate influence into the unfolding narrative. Confirming dinner reservations at Little Stacey, a restaurant I cherished and my mother adored, set the stage for a Halloween party hosted by Kimi herself.

In preparation for the gathering, I connected with my pole sisters – a group that had provided support while witnessing my journey through challenging times. Pippi and Devyn, unaware of the deeper struggles I faced, maintained their distance from the undercurrents shaping my reality. Riri, however, whose past actions had sparked doubt, remained an unpredictable figure in the unfolding story. The dynamics within these relationships reflected a web of tension and uncertainty, shaped by the driving forces of fear and greed that seemed to influence so many interactions.

Money, with its power to lead people down questionable paths, highlighted the challenges that greed could create. The upcoming Halloween Party at Little Stacey became a key moment – a meeting point where social interactions would unfold against the backdrop of unseen schemes. It was a chance to observe how different motivations shaped relationships and to navigate the tensions woven into the event's anticipation.

I recalled a lunch at Little Stacey in July 2022 with my mother and Aunt Sherrie. The conversation had touched on global power dynamics, revealing unsettling truths. While my mother claimed ignorance, her reaction sharply contrasted with the depth of our discussion. It was a reminder of how deception could seep into even the simplest moments, creating layers of complexity beneath everyday interactions.

As the Halloween Party drew closer, the unfolding events highlighted stark contrasts – moments of camaraderie and celebration against the persistent shadows shaping my reality. The restaurant, steeped in shared memories and guarded conversations, mirrored the complex dynamics of relationships, fear, and the pervasive influence of coercion. The journey pressed on, each step peeling back another layer of the intricate struggle within the shadows.

CHAPTER TWELVE

RESILIENCE AND FAREWELL

October 24, 2023

Hurrying from the Salt Mine to Little Stacey, the familiar hum of laughter and the clinking of silverware greeted me as I approached. The evening buzzed with energy, though my own plans had nearly gone awry when I forgot my dinner reservation with friends. Jazmine, always thoughtful, called just as I reached the restaurant. Her tone carried a blend of concern and curiosity as she asked if I was still joining. I quickly reassured her, promising to be there shortly.

Grabbing my black halo and the wings I had worn to a recent showcase at the Salt Mine, I felt a flicker of excitement for the night ahead. It was as if the universe had conspired to create an unexpected tale of connections – from a class at the Salt Mine to a last-minute gathering at Little Stacey.

When I arrived, the warm ambiance of Little Stacey greeted me, along with the eager faces of my friends. Kimi herself appeared, gracefully weaving through the tables to extend her regards. As we exchanged pleasantries, she shared the unexpected news of relocating the restaurant.

Resilience and Farewell

The construction along Highland Drive had taken an unforeseen toll on Little Stacey's business. Despite her resilience throughout the pandemic and the early phases of construction, it seemed she was no longer being compensated for the challenges her establishment faced. I couldn't help but admire her tenacity in weathering the storm up to this point.

The dinner unfolded as a buffet, a departure from Little Stacey's usual curated dining experience. To my dismay, the protein options were limited to beef. As I sampled the food, I couldn't shake the feeling that this was Little Stacey's most challenging buffet yet. The evening carried both a sense of celebration and a hint of sadness.

Amidst the noise, I reflected on the resilience embedded in Little Stacey's journey. She had stood strong through the uncertainties of a global pandemic and the disruption caused by the construction. However, the challenges seemed to have reached a tipping point, leading to the difficult decision to relocate.

As we shared our thoughts on the meal, I realized that this was not just about a buffet; it was a metaphorical feast of resilience and adaptation. Little Stacey's journey reflected the unpredictable rhythms of life, serving as a reminder of the challenges and changes that shape our paths.

The night continued with laughter, stories, and the unmistakable camaraderie of friends. We celebrated the evening and the bonds that had brought us together. Little Stacey's relocation, though bittersweet, marked the closing of one chapter and the opening of another.

As the clock ticked away and the night began to wane, we bid our farewells to Little Stacey and to each other. The uncertain future awaited, but we stepped into it with the knowledge that resilience and friendship would guide us through whatever challenges lay ahead.

With a graceful smile, Kimi thanked us for being part of her restaurant's journey. In her eyes, I saw a mixture of nostalgia, determination, and hope for the future. The construction along Highland Drive might have been disruptive, but it couldn't extinguish the spirit that had made Little Stacey a haven for so many.

With a final embrace and a promise to stay connected, we left, carrying with us the memories of that October evening. The road ahead might be uncertain, but the friendships forged from our collective struggles would always be strong.

And so, as the chapter closed on Little Stacey, it opened a new one for each of us. We walked into the night, our steps filled with a quiet resolve to face whatever lay ahead, guided by the lessons we had learned.

After dinner, the night extended its embrace as we decided to head to Devyn's house for an impromptu after-party. Heading home felt too soon, so the pull of shared moments with friends led us to continue our evening and the adventure together.

Gathered at Devyn's, surrounded by familiar faces that had brought support and joy, I took a moment to think about the paths that had led us here. Life, with all its twists and turns, had a way of revealing unexpected strength and resilience in the face of challenges.

That October evening, we embraced the changes, savoring the moment while recognizing the transitions yet to come. Little Stacey's restaurant, though moving to a new location, remained a cherished part of our shared history – a place where we had celebrated wins, endured challenges, and built lasting connections.

As the night wove its magic, we found peace in the company of friends who had become family. The idea of change was never left, but our shared laughter and experiences strengthened our connection, leaving us with lasting memories.

CHAPTER THIRTEEN

BENEATH THE SURFACE

November 1, 2023

I sent a text message to my office, telling them to call me if they needed anything. I still had to move some items out of my condo – a task I should have tackled earlier, but the trauma associated with the process made it unbearable until I was forced to do it by the sale. I also sent an email to a contact to help book the conference center for Molly Shane with the Institute of Real Estate – the same woman who had come into my office and warned me about the self-serving nature of people, especially in real estate. She also suggested I check the wheels on my office chair, which I had recently replaced.

Later that evening, I started a fire in my newly purchased fire pit. As the flames danced, I watched the yellow and green hues flicker and fight, mirroring the internal battles I faced.

As the fire burned and shadows moved across the yard, I reflected on the unseen influences shaping my life. Everyday tasks like emails and managing condo details kept me distracted from the deeper manipulations that had become part of my experience.

The text message to my office was a weak effort to regain some control over my life, a pointless act against the constant intrusion affecting everything around me. Even as I carried on with daily routines, I was fully aware of the ongoing threat in the background.

Emails and planning for the conference center felt like distractions, hiding the complex schemes that seemed aimed at breaking me down. Molly Shane's grim warning stayed with me – a reminder of how self-interested people in the real estate industry can be, with their hidden motives and secret plans.

Even something as simple as checking the wheels on my office chair carried weight. The chair, a symbol of stability and support, now reminded me how easily my independence could be threatened by forces beyond my control.

Yet, amidst the chaos and uncertainty, there was a glimmer of defiance – a spark of resilience that refused to be extinguished. As I watched the flames dance in the fire pit, I noticed the beauty in their bright yellow and green colors pushing back against the darkness.

Amid the challenges shaping my life, I found comfort in knowing I had a deep reserve of strength – a resilience that would help me face whatever lay ahead.

November 2, 2023

The fire pit's flames from last night were gone, but I still felt a spark of determination. Today, I changed my Google password again, a small but meaningful step toward regaining control over my life. It was a simple act of resistance against those trying to invade my privacy.

But it wasn't just my Google password I changed; I took the time to reset all my passwords, including my Microsoft password, which I defiantly changed to "KillBill2023!" It was a fitting choice, considering the bounty that had been put on my head – a reminder that I refused to be a pawn in someone else's game.

A specific memory flooded back to me – the same theme song playing in the background as I struggled to clean the remnants of Lucifer Yellow from my clothes. It had been a pointless effort, a never-ending struggle that only emphasized how ineffective my resistance was.

But today was different. As I changed my passwords and asserted my autonomy, I refused to be defeated. The echoes of past trauma might linger, but they no longer held sway over me. I was determined to escape the shadows that had trapped me and take back control of my life.

As I finished changing my passwords, a sense of empowerment washed over me. It was a small victory, but a victory nonetheless. I reaffirmed my commitment to unraveling the threads of coercion that had bound me for too long.

Looking ahead, I felt a new sense of determination. The challenges might continue, but I was no longer willing to stand by and watch. With my resolve and strength, I was ready to face whatever came my way, knowing that the darkness could never completely take away my inner strength.

November 3, 2023

As the sun rose on a new day, I sought peace in life's simple pleasures. Today, I embarked on a journey to pick up some honey from a local beekeeper – a small gesture, perhaps, but one full of meaning.

I bought the honey for myself and as a gift for my aunt and Devyn in anticipation of her upcoming event. She would be hosting her deceased daughter's sound bath the following day, November 4, 2023, and I wanted to offer a token of support and remembrance.

In choosing honey as a gift, I was reminded of the essential role bees play in our world. They are not merely insects but guardians of life, pollinating crops and nurturing the earth.In a world plagued by uncertainty and manipulation, they serve as beacons of resilience and hope.

But my decision to gift honey was about more than just honoring the bees – it was also a subtle act of defiance against those who seek to exploit and destroy them. I thought of Manny Flanner and his misguided attempts to collapse bee colonies through genetic modification and insecticide.

The French were among the first to recognize the dangers of Manny Flanner's actions, and their outrage echoed around the world. Just thinking about such complete disrespect for life made me feel angry and upset.

So, as I handed Devyn the jar of honey, I did so with a sense of purpose and determination. It was my way of standing in solidarity with the bees and all living creatures who have been victims of corporate greed and environmental degradation.

As Devyn accepted the gift with a grateful smile, I was reminded once again of the power of small gestures to make a difference. In the face of darkness and despair, the light of compassion and kindness guides us forward, illuminating the path to a brighter future.

Thinking about how everything is connected, I felt a sense of hope for the future. With just a jar of honey and a heart full of determination,

I was ready to face the challenges ahead, knowing that love will always overcome fear.

November 4, 2023, at 11:33 AM

As the clock ticked past mid-morning, the calm of the day was broken by the unmistakable sound of helicopters flying overhead. They circled twelve times, a constant noise that echoed through the walls of my new apartment.

Instinctively, I knew what this was – a blatant display of intimidation, a not-so-subtle reminder that I was being watched. But there was more to it than just intimidation; there was a message hidden within the deafening sound of the helicopter blades.

Were they trying to tell me to take videos of the chemtrails the government is producing, or was this simply another tactic to keep me in line? It was hard to say for sure, but one thing was clear: those in power were watching me closely.

And it wasn't just me they were targeting; they flew over my aunt and uncle's house all day, a constant presence in their lives as well. I sent them videos of the helicopters passing overhead, a reminder of the extent of the surveillance we were under.

My aunt Sherrie responded to my texts with resignation and defiance. "The other day over us, they flew all day 'til ours was overcast," she wrote. It was a chilling admission of the reality we found ourselves in – a reality where our every move was judged and monitored.

"I think they are targeting all of us," I replied, unease creeping into my words.

"The land of the free, the home of the brave," Sherrie remarked bitterly.

"You know they spray that shit everywhere," I confirmed, grimly acknowledging the truth we both knew all too well.

"I'll talk more about this when I get there," I assured her. "In the meantime, you and Reed should make a safe room and/or write your conversations down on paper. It's bigger than you think it is."

"But who is listening?" Sherrie asked.

"The Elite," I replied, the weight of those two words hanging heavy in the air.

"So much to talk about," Sherrie mused, resignation in her words.

"Yes, so much," I agreed. "The safe room will have a lot of picture frames with glass… or large pieces of artwork with glass."

"Or our lead paint?" Sherrie suggested a hint of gallows humor in her words.

November 6, 2023

The weight of unresolved matters hung heavy on my mind as I sent a message to Mosby, a tentative attempt to address the lingering issue of the acre of land that rightfully belonged to me. *"Hey Mosby, I'm just wondering when a good time for us would be to discuss me inheriting the acre of land that my other siblings have been granted, but I have not. Let me know when would be a good time to discuss that with you. Thanks."*

I hit send with a heavy heart, knowing deep down that I wouldn't get a response. And, just as expected, the silence dragged on – a stark reminder of how broken the justice system really is.

But even without a word from Mosby, life kept moving forward. Each day brought new challenges. I didn't have to appear in court on

November 2nd, and today, I got the final stipulated order – the plea deal my attorney pushed me to accept.

The order stated that I had to serve 45 days in an intensive outpatient program for drug abuse. However, knowing that time was crucial, I chose a PHP (Partially Hospitalized Patient) program instead – a condensed version that would let me finish in 30 days.

With a sense of resignation, I began the intake process with Bright Future Center, sending over my insurance information and preparing myself for the treatment I was being forced into. It was a tough pill to swallow, realizing that my autonomy had been stripped away once again. But I clung to the hope that this might be the first step toward reclaiming my life.

November 7, 2023

The day started with a mix of anticipation and nerves as I signed up for a dance class at the Salt Mine – something new, something different. Megan, the instructor, sent me a text, excited to see me, and I replied with the same enthusiasm, ready for this new adventure.

But when I got to the class, my excitement quickly turned to embarrassment. I realized I'd made a mistake – I was wearing the wrong shoes. Megan approached me with a curious look, asking if I was a pole dancer. It was one of those moments that could have been awkward, but instead, it made me laugh at the absurdity of it all.

Apparently, I should've worn smaller heels, but I wasn't going to let that stop me. With a determined smile, I decided to dance in my 8-inch heels anyway, embracing the challenge head-on.

The class flew by in a blur of movement and music, leaving me both exhausted and exhilarated. As I soaked in a bath afterward, easing my tired muscles, I felt a deep sense of satisfaction with how the day had turned out.

At 11:55 PM, just before the day ended, I sent a text to Mr. T – a nickname I'd given to Trevor. "Hey, Mr. T, I just wanted you to know that I gave your name and number to my private investigator to look into my case because you're the last person I've been close to for six months and the only one I've let into my new apartment. His name is Troy Peterson. Hopefully, you've got my back. Please talk to him. I hope you're doing well, and I'm glad you're in a better place now. Thank you."

Sending that text felt like taking a step into the unknown, trusting that Mr. T would support me in my search for truth and justice. It was a risk, but one I was willing to take to get the closure I desperately needed.

As I drifted off to sleep, I felt a sense of resolve – a determination to confront the shadows that had haunted me for far too long and to emerge stronger on the other side.

November 9, 2023

The weight of uncertainty hung in the air as I sat down with my private investigator to dig into the depths of my criminal case. Every moment felt charged with tension – the stakes were high.

I laid out the details of my ordeal, sharing everything with painstaking clarity. I spoke about Lucifer Yellow,[11] the substance that had infiltrated every part of my life, leaving destruction in its wake. I talked about the feeling of being chipped, the loss of control that haunts me to this day.

---

11. Scientific studies have shown that electric and magnetic fields can alter the fluorescence of certain dyes, like Lucifer Yellow, used in biomedical research to measure cell membrane permeability. In electroporation and magneto permeabilization protocols, changes in fluorescence indicate alterations in cell permeability due to external field exposure (EMF & LY).

Then there were moments of utter vulnerability – the times I found myself dancing in the makeup aisle at Walmart like a puppet controlled by forces I couldn't see.

As I talked, I could see the concern on the investigator's face. But I wasn't backing down. This was my reality, and I wasn't going to shy away from it.

We went over every detail, breaking down the web of lies and manipulation that had caught me. With each new discovery, I felt a spark of hope – maybe, just maybe, there was a way out of this nightmare.

But even as I shared my story, I knew the road ahead wouldn't be easy. The fight for justice would be tough, with no guarantees. Still, I wasn't going to let that stop me. With nothing but determination and resilience, I would keep fighting for the truth, no matter the cost.

As I said goodbye to my private investigator, I felt a renewed sense of purpose. The journey ahead might be long and difficult, but I was ready to face it head-on. Even in the shadows of coercion and control, there was still a spark of defiance – a hope that refused to die.

November 13, 2023

Walking into Bright Future Center for the first day of treatment felt like stepping into a new chapter – a chapter filled with uncertainty, challenges, and unexpected twists.

The reality of my situation hit hard as I handed over $1,800 to start a treatment I didn't want or need. It was a bitter reminder of the injustices in our healthcare system.

Looking around at the other patients, I realized I didn't relate to their stories. They were battling their own demons, while I felt like an outsider – a reluctant participant in a world that wasn't mine.

One woman noticed my discomfort and offered a bit of hope. "I know you don't want to be here, and it's messed up," she said, her voice filled with understanding. "But it'll go by faster than you think." I clung to her words, determined to make the most of my time at Bright Future. I decided to reframe the group sessions as "classes" in my mind, hoping to find some growth and self-discovery in the process.

Among all the unfamiliar faces, one person stood out -Lenox. He'd checked himself in for treatment, struggling with suicidal thoughts and depression. I found a kindred spirit in him, someone who understood the battle against inner demons.

Not being there for addiction recovery was a relief, allowing me to connect with Lenox on a deeper level. Our bond grew with each passing day, evolving into something more – a romance born out of shared struggles and mutual understanding. As our relationship blossomed, so did Lenox's role in my life, eventually leading him to write this book's preface – a testament to the power of love, resilience, and the human spirit.

November 22, 2023

The road stretched out before me as I drove to Union, Oregon, with Luxe, my cat, curled up beside me – a quiet comfort among the chaos of thoughts in my mind.

Thanksgiving weekend was here – a time for family, warmth, and finding peace in the embrace of loved ones. So, with a mix of exhaustion and hope, I headed to my aunt and uncle's house, seeking refuge from the storm raging inside me.

When I arrived, their warmth comforted me, offering a safe haven from the chaos. We sat down to share a meal, the glow of the fireplace softening the room as we talked and laughed.

But as the night wore on, I found myself opening up in ways I hadn't expected, sharing the details of my experiences with a raw vulnerability.

My uncle, with his gentle nature, struggled to take it all in. He asked questions – why wasn't the breaker outside the building locked? Why had the cops shown up so quickly to arrest me?

Then, a moment of clarity hit him. He remembered seeing Trust Documents on my grandfather's table – a detail that suddenly made everything click. His sister, the eldest of five, had been changing the trust paperwork for my grandfather's estate – a discovery that shocked everyone in the room.

At that moment, the puzzle pieces fell into place, revealing a web of deceit and manipulation that extended far beyond my own experience. As the truth began to unravel, I felt a sense of relief – a flicker of hope in the darkness.

Together, we vowed to uncover the truth and fight for justice with everything we had. As we held hands in solidarity, I knew that no matter what lay ahead, we would face it together – as a family, united in our search for truth and redemption.

November 26, 2023

As the days passed in a blur of uncertainty, I turned to the digital world for some relief – a way to escape the chaos overwhelming me. That's when I found a video from Dr. Kathrine Horton about being chipped – a stark reminder of the conspiracy that had entrapped me.

Knowing they shared the same fears and uncertainties, I sent the video to my aunt and uncle. We had talked about the possibility of being chipped during my Thanksgiving visit, a conversation that left us all feeling uneasy.

Meanwhile, Reed, my steadfast partner in this search for truth, sent me a text that gave me chills: "Have you read the book by Jain Liang?" he asked. "I found it on that link you sent about EMF, Mk Ultra Controlled."

His message opened up a flood of questions that left me overwhelmed. Had I found the key to uncovering the truth behind the lies that had trapped me? Only time would tell.

November 29, 2023

Justice moved frustratingly slowly as I met my attorney at the courthouse to enter my not-guilty plea for the charge weighing heavily on me. The moment was tense, a silent reminder of the challenges still ahead.

Even as I faced the challenge of dealing with the legal system, there was a small sign of hope. My next criminal hearing, originally set for December 22, 2023, had been rescheduled to February 28, 2024, at 1:00 PM – a minor win against the odds.

As I left the courthouse, I felt a strong sense of determination – a resolve to face the challenges ahead with strength and courage. Even in the midst of control and pressure, there was still a spark of defiance and hope that refused to fade.

With my head held high and my hope renewed by the possibility of a better future, I moved forward into the unknown, prepared to face whatever challenges lay ahead on my journey to redemption.

CHAPTER FOURTEEN

FINDING SANCTUARY AND PURPOSE

December 1, 2023

Amid chaos and uncertainty, The Salt Mine became my refuge. Pole classes, especially, offered a sanctuary where I could escape the weight of the world. On a particularly overwhelming day, I found comfort in a floor movement and choreography class with Jess.

Jess pushed me out of my comfort zone, guiding me through intricate steps and fluid movements. The adrenaline rush was familiar, but this time, it came with a sense of clarity I hadn't felt in a long time. For me, pole class was more than just a workout – it was a mental escape, a chance to focus solely on the present and drown out the noise of the outside world.

But something else stirred within me that day – an idea that took root and grew into something much bigger. I decided to write a book, a chronicle of my fight for freedom and a testament to resilience in the face of adversity.

Determined, I reached out to Katte, an author whose work I admired, knowing her recommendations for a publisher would be invaluable. This decision to follow her guidance would prove to be one of the best choices I'd ever made, setting me on a path that would change my life forever.

On December 6, 2023, I signed up for another pole class with Mel. Her text read, "I have you in my Pole in Platform Stilettos at 6 PM tonight!!!! Wear leggings or long socks, layers are perfect for tonight. We want cozy. Warm. Feel good. It's going to be an experience! We'll be slinking around the floor and moving our bodies with intention. We'll be using all our senses and focusing on being in our bodies. This is going to be a weird one, but weird is the BEST!!!" And it truly was! We explored how your senses can be a coping mechanism for triggers. If you're open to it, the universe always gives you what you need.

Feeling empowered by my pole classes and the clarity I'd gained from processing groups at Bright Future, I made a series of pivotal decisions that would shape my healing journey. One of those was to participate in a showcase at The Salt Mine, scheduled for the end of February. With determination, I paid the enrollment fee and chose my song: "YES MOM," which I later changed to "Apology" by Dana Dentata – a declaration of defiance against the forces that aimed to hold me back.

Dancing to express my anger became a release – a chance to channel my emotions into something beautiful and transformative. As I choreographed my routine, I poured everything into each movement, letting the music carry me away.

But my healing didn't stop there. Prompted by questions from Brooklyn, my therapist at Bright Future, I made the difficult decision to cut ties with toxic relationships, including those with my ex-parents and children. Firing my own children was painful, but I knew it was the right choice for my well-being. I'd done it before after my daughter's passing, and now, it was necessary again. Some bonds, no matter how cherished, are meant to be broken.

As I voiced this decision to Brooklyn, a sense of peace washed over me. Despite the pain, I knew I was taking the necessary steps to reclaim my autonomy and move forward.

In the dance studio and therapy sessions alike, I found sanctuary – a space to confront my demons, let go of the burdens of the past, and emerge stronger and more resilient.

December 7, 2023

Returning to Forest Dale to retrieve my scooter felt like stepping back into the past – a reminder of the life I'd left behind and the challenges I'd overcome. When I arrived, Allen Golden, my old neighbor and a steadfast friend, was there to greet me.

We set to work replacing the battery in my scooter – a task that seemed mundane but carried a deeper significance. As we fixed the scooter, the elevator emitted an unsettling hum that sent a shiver down Allen's spine. His reaction spoke volumes, reminding me of the sinister forces that still lurked in the shadows.

In that moment, my thoughts turned to Peter "Cunty" Pottinger, the man whose actions had left a permanent mark on my life. His presence lingered like a ghost, a constant reminder of the struggles I was still fighting to overcome.

Lenox, dependable as always, drove me to Forest Dale and back, offering his support in a way that genuinely moved me. It was one of the first times I'd gathered the courage to ask for help, prepared for the possibility of rejection. Instead, Lenox's immediate "yes" reminded me that kindness and generosity could still be found, even amid challenges.

As we made our way back home, I reflected on the journey that had brought me here. The sessions at Bright Future had forged bonds of trust I thought were impossible. With Lenox, I found a confidant – someone who willingly shared my burdens and stood by me without hesitation.

Encouraged by his unwavering support, I invited Lenox to a White Elephant gift exchange I was hosting for my Pole Sisters and their significant others on December 15th. It was a small gesture, but it symbolized the friendships and solidarity that had flourished despite the turbulence around me.

Looking ahead, I felt optimistic – believing that, no matter the trials to come, I would face them head-on, strengthened by those who stood beside me.

December 18, 2023

On my last day at Bright Future, I felt a sense of freedom wash over me tinged with a bittersweet sense of nostalgia. I met with two women from Bright Future for a farewell lunch, reflecting on the journey we had shared and our progress.

In addiction recovery, receiving a coin is symbolic – a token of the milestones reached and battles won. But Lenox and I, not being part of the traditional program, didn't receive such tokens. And that was fine with us. Our victory wasn't in recognition, but in the quiet strength we found within ourselves.

With Bright Future behind me, I focused on my business – a venture that had been delayed by family interference. Their attempts to sabotage me only fueled my determination. They underestimated a woman who had survived losing her daughter, a woman whose spirit couldn't be broken.

As I threw myself into completing the software conversion for my business and ramping up marketing efforts, I did so with fierce determination. I wasn't just fighting for my business's success but for survival in a world that sought to tear me down.

With a defiant grin, I embraced my role as the Queen of the Streets – a force to be reckoned with, ready to conquer whatever challenges lay ahead. You don't mess with a woman who's stared into the abyss and emerged stronger. And you definitely don't mess with a Scorpio Rising.

XOXO, Kimberly Mosby
Queen of the Streets

THE END.

VALUABLE SUPPORT AND GUIDANCE FOR READERS

I have listed a small number of vital resources below, but for the most complete and up to date list of resources, education and information on targeted individuals and the methods which can be used against people, please visit: https://unveilingshadows.com/resources

What is a Targeted Individual?

The diagram below is one of many resources on www.targetedjustice.com.

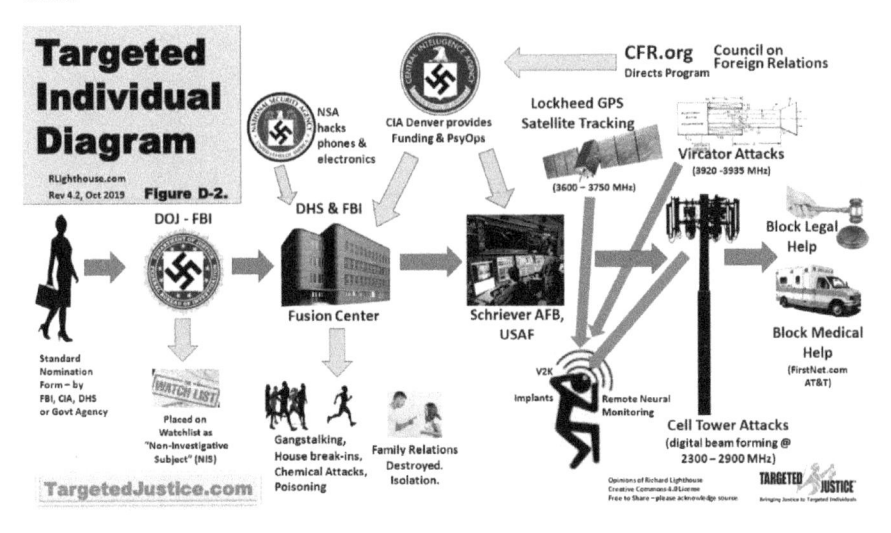

ALL OF THESE RESOURCES ARE LINKED AND CLICKABLE AT

https://unveilingshadows.com/resources

1. National Institute of Neurological Disorders and Stroke

(NINDS) Website: https://www.ninds.nih.gov/ NINDS provides comprehensive information and resources on various neurological disorders, including those related to bio and neurological warfare.

3. Centers for Disease Control and Prevention (CDC) - Emergency Preparedness and Response Website: https://www.cdc.gov/phpr/ The CDC offers information on emergency preparedness and response, including resources for coping with bio-threats and their potential neurological impacts.

4. International Committee of the Red Cross (ICRC) - Biological Weapons and Public Health Website: https://www.icrc.org/en/what-we-do/biological-weapons The ICRC provides insights into the humShannarian consequences of biological warfare and offers support for victims through various programs.

5. National Alliance on Mental Illness (NAMI) Website: https://www.nami.org/ NAMI offers resources and support for individuals dealing with mental health challenges resulting from traumatic experiences, including those related to bio and neurological warfare.

6. International Society for Traumatic Stress Studies (ISTSS) Website: https://www.istss.org/ ISTSS offers resources, research, and support for individuals affected by traumatic events, including those with neurological consequences.

7. Brain & Behavior Research Foundation Website:https://www.bbrfoundation.org/
This foundation funds research on mental health and brain disorders, including those resulting from traumatic experiences such as bio and neurological warfare.

8. Trauma Recovery Center (TRC) Website: https://www.healthright360.org/program/trauma-recovery-center-trc TRC provides comprehensive trauma-informed care, including support services for individuals affected by trauma-related neurological issues.

9. The Survivor's Trust Website: https://www.thesurvivorstrust.org/
This organization offers support services, advocacy, and resources for survivors of various forms of abuse, including those related to bio and neurological warfare.

10. National Domestic Violence Hotline Website: https://www.thehotline.org/ This hotline provides confidential support, information, and resources for individuals experiencing domestic violence, which may include forms of coercive control.

11. Directed Energy Weapons: https://www.gao.gov/products/gao-23-106717

12. https://rumble.com/v4pai8o-episode-94-truth-seekers-radio-show-wana-toledo-targeted-justice.html

15. Neuro-Weapons: https://x.com/hal_9_thousand_/status/1788827255470187006?s=43

16. FULL VERSION of above Neuro Weapons:
https://www.youtube.com/watch?v=LCYH_K850Lw

Top Websites for More Information about Coercive Control and Targeted Individuals

I do not guarantee the existence of these sites. Things change quickly.

StopGangstalkingCrimes.com

Mind-Control-News.de

TargetedIndividualsCanada.com

RLighthouse.com

Trance-Formation.com

Pactsntl.org

JusticeForAllCitizens.com

TargetedAmerica.com

TargetedEvidence.com

Zersetzung.org

TargetedMassachusetts.org

GovSponsoredStalking.info

MKultraGirl.org

FreedomForTargetedIndividuals.org

DataAsylum.com

verydayConcerned.net

MikrowellenTerror.de

Bruleparlesillumines.e-monsite.com

Organized-stalking-and-mind-control.ch

Gangstalkingsurfers.wordpress.com

E-waffen.de

USA-anti-communist.com

MindControlinSweden.wordpress.com

Ovadosepeace.wordpress.com

Gangstalking.wordpress.com

MindControl.se

StopEG.com

Targeted-Individuals.co.uk

www.ingramcontent.com/pod-product-compliance
Ingram Content Group UK Ltd.
Pitfield, Milton Keynes, MK11 3LW, UK
UKHW050646110225
4543UKWH00033B/422